ENDORSEMENT...

I greatly enjoyed reading *Embracing Life to the Full – Essentials for Christian Living*, authored by K. T. Koshy. While my wife and I with family were providentially placed in Durham, UK in connection with our studies and ministry between 2007-2010, we served our great God together with Koshy and Mary, his wife. What stuck to my mind was his enthusiasm for exemplifying the eternal truth of the Word of God in his personal and family life.

Embracing life in its fullness is easier said than done, when we encounter the various vicissitudes and disappointments in life. The divine life, however, will empower one to swim against the current, hope against all hope. It is the triumph of faith against all mortal fear and a firm assurance of trust in the sovereignty of God who is in absolute control of all our situations. This, I believe, is what Koshy wants to communicate to his readers. His experience is surely a living testimony to this effect. In spite of his disability and pain, his heart remained faithful to God, and he aims at the highest and achieve the same.

Several years ago, Koshy expressed his passion of being a great blessing to others by enabling them to be rooted in the word of God. My wife Dr. Susan Mathew joins me in congratulating Koshy for this timely and much needed book, covering a comprehensive range of foundational themes in a single volume. *Embracing Life to the Full* is an open invitation to the seekers of Truth, a map for new believers who want to explore further into the Christian faith, nourishing food for established believers, a comprehensive guide to students and teachers of the Word and effective tool for evangelists. Firmly based on the Scripture, focussed on spiritual formation, aimed at practical Christian life, this book offers a special reading experience.

I pray that God would lead many to embrace and experience life in its fullness through this book.

Rev. Dr. Mathew C. Vargheese
Dean of Post Graduate Studies &
Professor of Christian Theology
Faith Theological Seminary, Manakala
Kerala, India.

Dedication

This book is dedicated:
Primarily to the Shepherd and Overseer of my soul
and the Lord of my life, Jesus Christ Himself;

To my beloved, loyal and godly woman, my wife, Mary;
To our precious children and granddaughter – Helen and
her husband Robert; Paul and his wife Fungying, and
Daniella Joy, who is such a treasure.

I have learned much from my family – their devotion,
love and commitment to the Lord – and they have greatly
influenced my own walk with the Lord;

To Pat Smith, a spiritual giant who, prompted by the Holy Spirit,
ministered to me every day for six months, when I was
incapacitated in bed following an unsuccessful back operation.
I learnt at firsthand about the gentle, yet powerful,
ministry of prayer through her during this period; and

In loving memory of my late father, Tharian Koshy; his love
for the Word of God, his prayer life and his passion for divine healing
influenced me from a very younger age.

Embracing Life to the Full
Essentials for Christian Living

K.T.Koshy

Embracing Life to the Full
by K. T. Koshy

Copyright © 2013 K. T. Koshy
Published by K. T. Koshy

Eight chapters of this book were published by K. T. Koshy in 2011
under the same title as a pilot work.

ISBN 978-0-9576723-0-7

The author can be contacted by email on
koshyandmary@gmail.com

Printed and bound in India by Authentic Media, Secunderabad - 500 067
E-mail : printing@ombooks.org

CONTENTS

ACKNOWLEDGEMENTS

No man is an island and no successful book is a solo effort. My wife, Mary, worked with me throughout to develop the manuscript for this book; without her assistance it would not have been written. My heart-felt thanks go to both Helen and Paul, our children who scrutinised this manuscript and improved it. Without their help it would not have been completed. I was particularly inspired by Helen and her husband, Robert, who have been successfully running a foundation course for new believers in Germany for a number of years.

I would like to express my sincere appreciation and gratitude to my son, Paul, who kindly provided the chapter on 'God's Covenant' and Appendix 1, 'The Role of the Bible in Embracing Life to the Full', and contribution for 'Power of Prayer'. I am thankful for the contributions of John Kamara and Steve Foreman for their sermons on 'The Trinity' and 'Second Coming', respectively, at International Harvest Church Newcastle. I would like to record my sincere thanks to Rev. Dr. Robert Ward for kindly writing Foreword and Rev. Dr. Mathew Varghese for the Endorsement to the book; Rev. Renjit Ambanattu Samuel for his support and prayer, and the OM Books team for their invaluable help in printing.

Invariably one is influenced by the writings of others and the Holy Bible itself in any study, and some of them even become part of one's own work. Let me hasten to add, however, that I alone am responsible for whatever shortcomings the final version of this book may have.

FOREWORD

I thank God for this amazing book! Each chapter contains a perfectly Biblical and straightforward presentation – revelation, really – of the deep life-changing truth of the glorious kingdom that the Lord Jesus Christ has ushered in.

Koshy has included the key Scriptures in full – rather than a mere chapter and verse references – which makes this presentation so much more thrilling and accessible.

To slowly read each chapter – pausing to pray and meditate on each aspect and emphasis – is a wonderfully and enriching experience. It is to marinade the heart, soul and mind in the life-giving truths of God's love and purposes for us and the world He loves so much.

Spread out before us is all we need to grasp the foundations of the Christian faith, and to live the abundant life Jesus promised to all who follow Him. This book is perfect to the newest believer, the established disciple of Jesus and it is most certainly a great encouragement to the teacher and leader of God's people, reminding them as it does, of all they have to pass on to those whose care we will one day have to give account for.

It is perfect for personal devotion and for group study. In short, I have not come across a book quite like this one – one which so faithfully and succinctly presents 'the whole counsel of God'. If, as St. Paul says, we are to be 'transformed by the renewing of our mind', then this book, *Embracing Life to the Full*, is a practical tool in the hands of the believer who is following Jesus and is open to the revelation and inspiration of the Holy Spirit. Such one will not regret spending time in its pages!

Rev. Dr. Robert Ward
LLB DD Barrister-at-Law
Doctor of Divinity, Madras Bible Institute
Vicar, St. Luke's Church, Newcastle upon Tyne

PREFACE

Some years ago, God impressed this mandate upon me: 'Tell my people, I love them'. Since that time, I have endeavoured to communicate this message faithfully, in words and in action, and now in writing. In 2011, I felt stirred by the Lord to put into print some essential truths that are fundamental and foundational for enjoying life as God intended.

The Bible is a grand book, a rich tapestry, but its overall message is one of God's love for us, and of His determined fashion and plan to rescue us from our sins and bring us to Himself. Within it, God holds out an invitation to know Him and to experience life to the full, and He has graciously made every provision available for us to do so.

Embracing Life to the Full unpacks, with both simplicity and depth, a carefully chosen range of themes that are Biblical essentials for effective Christian living. These truths, which have been worked out in personal experience as well as taught to others, have proven effective in seeing people established in their life and faith in the Lord Jesus. Firmly rooted in the Bible, this book lends itself to further personal study, and also acts as a resource for sharing these essentials with others.

I have personally found that there is a lack of literature that brings together fundamental and practical Christian truths in a single volume that is thorough yet accessible. This book endeavours to fill this gap. It aims to communicate the gospel and to help to disciple and strengthen the Body of Christ in order that we can fulfil the mission of Christ in the world.

This book is unique in bringing together a wide range of important Biblical themes that are essential for the Christian life for new believers, layperson and leaders alike. These fundamental themes will help readers discover, share and deepen their Christian faith and explore spirituality leading to maturity. Each chapter is comprehensive, yet simple and concise. It is written based on the Biblical principle that 'Scripture interprets Scripture' and well supported with Scripture throughout. Hence there should be no confusion for the readers.

This book covers certain themes that are often seen as complex and makes them more accessible, for example the church, the New Covenant, Joy of Forgiveness, God's Grace, Jesus Christ as a Redeemer and Lord, the Trinity, the Kingdom of God and the Second Coming of Christ.

The style of this book is purposely designed to be of the greatest value to the reader. It conveys Bible truths and spiritual principles in a clear, readable style, avoiding a scholarly approach, in order to assist and attract laypersons, whatever their current level of Biblical knowledge and understanding. This book, however, will also be useful to theological students, ministers, pastors and evangelists for teaching, preaching and in the discipleship of new believers. Thus, it is both an evangelical tool for evangelism and discipleship and a devotional manual for personal spiritual growth.

This book will supply a long-felt need for a single volume book covering a comprehensive range of foundational themes.

This book is aimed at:

Unbelievers who are seeking to know God or understand the Christian faith: This is the starting point in this book, namely, God's invitation into a new life and relationship with Him.

New Believers: who need to know the major themes of Christ's teaching and the New Testament and how to apply them in order to grow in the faith.

Established Believers: to help them live the life God has purposed for them and to provide a resource for them to help guide others.

Leaders: as a resource for discipleship and training.

It is my prayer that this book will be used by God to help the reader to grow and mature in their Christian faith, to more fully enjoy God and the life He has for them, and also as a resource for those seeking to help others enjoy the same. It is also hoped that this book will be read and re-read until, with well worn covers and pages having served its purpose well, it is passed on to another.

Koshy Tharayil KOSHY

Chapter 1

GOD'S INVITATION – THE NEW BIRTH

Praise be to the God and Father of our Lord Jesus Christ! In his great mercy he has given us new birth into a living hope through the resurrection of Jesus Christ from the dead. (1 Peter 1:3)

Introduction

God has created us to have fellowship with Him, to walk with Him, to enjoy friendship with Him and to have a heart after His own heart. There is nothing that takes precedence in our lives over our fellowship with God. From the beginning to the end, this was and is God's great desire – to have people with whom He can have a relationship. God loves us and wants us to know and enjoy Him, as well as experience life to the full both now and in eternity. As Jesus said, "I have come that they may have life, and have it to the full", John 10:10. But we do have a problem:

Our Sin Separates Us from God

The Bible tells us that we have a problem that stands in the way of us knowing God and enjoying peace with Him. It is the problem of sin. Sin is our wrongdoing against God, that independent attitude and rebellion against God.

The Bible says that, "All have sinned and fall short of the glory of God", Romans 3:23. We are all sinful by nature because we are born into a sinful world. Furthermore, God gave us a will and the freedom to choose and we have all made choices to disobey God and go our own wilful way. "We all, like sheep, have gone astray, each of us has turned to his own way", Isaiah 53:6a. Sin is universal condition, and every person is sinful by nature and by choice.

The result of sin in our own lives is separation from God, slavery and death. The Bible says, "But your iniquities have separated you from your God; your sins have hidden his face from you...", Isaiah 59:2. Jesus said, "I tell you the truth, everyone who sins is a slave to sin", John 8:34. "For the wages of sin is death", Romans 6:23a. Furthermore, we know that God is Holy. No sin will ever enter His presence, "for righteousness and justice are the foundation of his throne", Psalm 97:2.

How then can we enter into this relationship with God when our sins separate us from him?

God's Remedy for Our Problem

"By this gospel [message of good news] you are saved... that Christ died for our sins according to the Scriptures, and that he was buried, that he was raised on the third day, according to the Scriptures", 1 Corinthians 15:2-4. Though He was God's sinless Son, Jesus became a human, died on the cross to pay the penalty for our sin and rose again from the dead. John 3:16 says, "For God so loved the world that he gave his one and only Son, that whoever believes in him shall not perish but have eternal life". By this act – motivated by love – the Lord Jesus Christ bridged the gap between God and us. "This is love: not that we loved God, but that he loved us and sent his Son as an atoning sacrifice for our sins", 1 John 4:10. "But God demonstrates his own love for us in this: While we were still sinners, Christ died for us", Romans 5:8.

Jesus' purpose in dying for us is to bring us into a relationship with God. "For Christ died for sins once for all, the righteous for the unrighteous, to bring you to God", 1 Peter 3:18. God has provided the only way to forgiveness of sins and eternal life with Him. Just as sin is a universal problem, Jesus is the universal Saviour – He is a Saviour for all who respond to Him and put their trust in Him. As we make that right response to Jesus and what He has done for us, something supernatural takes place in our heart and in our lives that only God can bring about – it is called the new birth.

The New Birth

God invites each one of us to embrace the new birth, for it is the doorway into the life that God has purposed for us. The new birth, also known as the 'born again' experience, is a must for every person. Without experiencing the new birth we cannot enter into right relationship with God. The new birth is a spiritual miracle that happens only when we turn round from our old ways of thinking and living and turn to follow Jesus as we trust in Him and what He has done for us through His birth, death and resurrection. The apostle Peter said to the people in Acts 3:19, "Repent, then, and turn to God, so that your sins may be wiped out, that times of refreshing may come from the Lord."

True repentance includes a change of mind. It is recognition that we have been going the wrong way, and a decision to turn from our own way of life to going God's way. Only God can change the heart, but we must be willing to change our mind in response to the good news about Jesus Christ. The new birth is very personal, and it is necessary before we can claim and enjoy any of the benefits of the blessings from God that the Bible tells us He wants to give us. Jesus said to Nicodemus, a religious leader who was searching for the truth, "I tell you the truth, no-one can see the kingdom of God unless he is born again", John 3:3. Jesus reminded him again in verse 7 saying, "You must be born again." Jesus was explaining the importance of spiritual re-birth, saying that people don't enter the kingdom of God by living a better life, but by being spiritually born again (born from above).

You Must Be Born Again

What does this mean? When we were born in the natural, we inherit many physical and personality traits from our parents. To be born again means to be born of God, and John 1:13 affirms this truth to us: "Children born not of natural descent, nor of human decision or a husband's will, but born of God." This means God becomes our Father.

Many people will be familiar with 'The Lord's prayer' from the Bible in which we address God as 'Our Father'. But we do this most often by virtue of being born into a Christian home. However, in reality, this does not mean anything unless and until we are born again. John 1:12 tells us that it is "to all who received him [Jesus], to those who believed in his name, he [Jesus] gave the right to become children of God." What an awesome privilege we have in Christ Jesus.

For this miracle to happen in our lives, the Bible tells us, we need to do something from our side. First of all, we need to admit, each one personally and wholeheartedly, that we are born naturally with a sinful nature within us and we have all sinned against God. Romans 3:23 tells us that "all have sinned and fall short of the glory of God." It is crucial for us to get out of this condition, but we cannot do this by ourselves. However, God, through His master plan of salvation and out of His great love for us, has made the way for us. He sent His one and only Son Jesus to take the horrendous punishment we rightly deserved for our wrongdoings and rebellion against God; He did this in order to set us free from our sinfulness and bring us to God.

From our part we must take the opportunity by turning around and start a life of following Jesus. This is a response of trusting in Jesus and accepting what He has done for us on the cross, when he took our sins on to Himself and died in our place. This means we can walk free and enjoy the relationship with our Father in heaven. 1 Peter 2:24 tells us, "He [Jesus] himself bore our sins on His body on the tree, so that we might die to sin and live for righteousness…" Peter goes on to say in verse 25, "You were like sheep going astray, but now you have returned to the shepherd and overseer of your soul."

It is a personal decision and action we take, because of the action that God first took: "God demonstrates his own love for us in this: While we were still sinners, Christ died for us", Romans 5:8. God took the initiative towards us for every person. It is up to us to take advantage of this wonderful free gift from our loving God. So many people are lost and wandering and looking in the wrong places, because no one has told them or heard this miracle-working truth of God.

Something miraculous happens to us when we sincerely make this decision: We become a new creation; newly created by the power of the Holy Spirit. 2 Corinthians 5:17 tells us therefore that,

"If anyone is in Christ, he is a new creation; the old has gone, the new has come!" We don't want anyone to deceive us and make us to think that you can have eternal life by following certain religious rituals or doing good works. God paid the highest price in order to save every person from sin and eternal death.

Eternal life is God's life embodied in Christ Jesus given to all believers now as a guarantee that they will live forever. In eternal life there is no death, sickness, oppression, evil or sin. None of us want to miss out on receiving eternal life. If you have never trusted Christ, let this promise of everlasting life be yours and believe. To believe means to put our trust and confidence in Jesus that He alone can save us. It is to put the Lord Jesus Christ in charge of our lives. Now is your opportunity to make that decision! If you are not sure that you are already done so, you can receive this life by faith in Christ Jesus. You can do this, even right now, by responding to the good news about Jesus by:

Admitting your need – that you are a sinner in need of God's forgiveness. The greatest sin is not trusting and believing in Jesus. It is commendable to agree with God that we are lost sinners, unable to save ourselves, and that we need Him to save us.

Believing – that Jesus Christ died for your sins and has paid the full price for you to be forgiven and come into a true relationship with God as your Father.

Asking – God to forgive you of all your sin and wrongdoing, and to be your Saviour.

Receiving – Jesus Christ now as Lord and Saviour, and trusting in Him alone for forgiveness and eternal life. Thank Him and trust Him that he has done what you have asked for.

Confessing Jesus Christ as Lord – "If you confess with your

mouth, 'Jesus is Lord', and believe in your heart that God raised him from the dead, you will be saved", Romans 10:9. The Bible's way of making that confession of Jesus as Lord is to be baptised in water, as a firm step of faith in and commitment to the Lord.

Prayer of Commitment

Come to Jesus Christ today and pray:

"Dear Lord Jesus, thank you for making it possible for me to find peace with God. Lord God, I come to you in the name of Jesus. I admit that I am a sinner. Now I repent of my sins and turn away from my selfish ways. I thank you for allowing Jesus to take my punishment and forgive my sins. Lord Jesus, please come into my heart and be my Lord and Saviour. I choose to follow you all the days of my life. Thank you for the gift of eternal life. Amen."

If you have prayed this prayer with conviction in your heart, you have received Jesus as your Saviour, you have started a new life with Him, and you are now a part of God's family.

Future Christian Walk

Does this mean we are perfect or that we will never sin again? Don't give up on yourself or God in case you have done something wrong to displease God after having born again. The apostle John, who had the privilege to walk and talk with Jesus physically on this earth, said this to us: "If we confess our sins, he is faithful and just and will forgive us our sins and purify us from all unrighteousness", 1 John 1:9.

The Bible also tells us that we have an advocate in heaven, the risen Lord Jesus Christ, who intercedes for us. But don't make a habit of sinning. Sin separates us from God. Deliberately choosing our way instead of God's is a serious thing. When we deliberately sin, we grieve the heart of the Father God who loves us and has a wonderful plan for our lives; we grieve the Saviour who died for us and delivered us from the power of Satan; we grieve the Holy Spirit who lives in us and gave us new birth. Deliberate wrongdoing also hurts and hinders the people of God.

But the Christian life is much more than not sinning. It is a positive walk and relationship with our God and our Lord, one that we are to treasure and invest in. To help us grow in the Christian life, as with all relationships, we need to spend time with God; we do this by regularly studying His Word, the Bible, as well as communicating with Him in worship and prayer, and also by being part of a church where the truth of God is taught and preached. Try to tell at least one other person the decision you have taken to follow Jesus, and then to cultivate a lifestyle of sharing who Jesus is in your life to others. Practising these things will help you to grow in your Christian life.

For the Undecided

The signs show that Jesus' return is very imminent. Before the door of grace is shut won't you take the opportunity and receive Jesus into your life and accept Him as your Lord and Saviour. If you are still in doubt, would you consider to make the following commitment, as worded by Dr. R. A. Torrey, "I promise to examine carefully the evidence that the Bible is God's book, and Jesus Christ is God's Son and man's Saviour; and if I find reason to believe that this book is true and He is man's Saviour, I will accept Him and confess Him before men, and undertake to follow Him"[1]. I believe that as you take this step, God will reveal Himself to you in a real and personal way.

Concluding Remarks

In conclusion, let us briefly note twelve aspects of the new birth:

It is not a natural or a physical birth, but a supernatural birth from above (John 1:13; 1 John 3:9).

We are born again (regenerated) by the Word of God (1 Peter 1:23).

At the new birth, our sins are forgiven, and we are cleansed by the Blood of Jesus (1 John 1:7-9).

At the new birth, we are redeemed [bought back] (1 Peter 1:18-19).

At the new birth, we are saved from spiritual death and judgement, and granted eternal life (John 5:24).

At the new birth, we are crucified with Christ and thus delivered from the dominion of sin, by which we had been enslaved (Romans 6:6).

At the new birth we receive eternal life (John 3:16).

At the new birth we are justified, that means, brought into a right relationship with God (Romans 5:9).

At the new birth, we are reconciled to the Father (Colossians 1:21-22).

At the new birth, we become children of God, by being born into the family of God (John 1:12).

At the new birth, we see the kingdom of God (John 3:3).

At the new birth, we are only newborn babes, spiritual infants, and we are to grow to maturity through our relationship with Jesus.

The new birth is the doorway into life in Christ Jesus. However, it is only the first step. There are two other essential steps (or provisions) given by the Lord Jesus Himself that are necessary if we are to enjoy life to the full as God intended. These two steps are covered in the next two chapters.

Chapter 2

A NEW START – BAPTISM

Whoever believes and is baptised will be saved, but
whoever does not believe will be condemned. (Mark 16:16)

Introduction

Christian denominations differ in the doctrine concerning water baptism. Many have not practised baptism as Jesus and His apostles taught and modelled for us to follow. Baptism is not optional after thought. Baptism is extremely significant in the life of a believer. In this chapter, let us study together to look at why is it necessary to be baptised, what its Biblical foundation is and what it signifies?

What Is Baptism?

Baptism is one of the two ordinances (the other is the Lord's Supper) that Jesus gave to His disciples whereby they could show their allegiance to Him. The word 'baptism' is taken or derived from the Greek word *baptizo*, and understanding its meaning from the original language helps to explain what it entails. It literally means to immerse, plunge or dip something into liquid; it is much more than sprinkling with water. Baptism has been described as 'an outward sign of an inward faith'. This is a simple but helpful definition. Faith is an invisible, intangible thing and, as the book of James indicates, faith needs to be expressed in action (2:14-17). Baptism is the action that Jesus gave us to express our faith in the Lord and the decision to follow Him.

Who Preached Baptism First?

We do not see any trace of baptism having been administered in the Old Testament until the days of John the Baptist. The Bible says that "Before the Coming of Jesus, John preached repentance and baptism to all the people of Israel", Acts 13:24. John the Baptist was only a forerunner of Christ to prepare a people for Christ; his main ministry was to preach repentance (Matthew 3:6), to baptise those who sincerely repented, confessing their sins, and to preach Christ to them. "I baptise you with water for repentance. But after me will come one who is more powerful than I, …He will baptise you with the Holy Spirit and with fire," Matthew 3:11. He baptised them in the river Jordan. We read, "Now John also was baptising at Aenon near Salim, because there was plenty of water, and people were constantly coming to be baptised", John 3:23.

The Baptism of Jesus – Jesus Modelled Baptism

Jesus needed no baptism, because He was sinless. He was the holy Son of God. There was nothing He had to repent of. Why then did He take baptism? The Bible says, "Then Jesus came from Galilee to the Jordan to be baptised by John. But John tried to deter him, saying, 'I need to be baptised by you, and do you come to me?' Jesus replied, 'Let it be so now; it is proper for us to do this to fulfil all righteousness'. Then John consented. As soon as Jesus was baptised he went up out of the water. At that moment heaven was opened, and he saw the Spirit of God descending like a dove and lighting on him. And a voice from heaven said, 'This is my Son, whom I love; with him I am well pleased'", Matthew 3:13-17.

Jesus was baptised 'to fulfil all righteousness'; that is, to do all that God required of Him. He was both consecrating Himself to God and identifying Himself with sinful humanity, for whom He was later to die. Christ had to fulfil all the demands of the law in order to deliver us from the curse of the law (Galatians 4:4-5). Furthermore He had to carefully set an example for us, His followers, that we might follow Him in the new and living way. From the birth of the church on the day of Pentecost, John's baptism has been replaced by the New Testament baptism (Christian baptism or believer's baptism), as a direct commandment from Jesus Christ.

Jesus Practised Baptism

"After this, Jesus and His disciples went out into the Judean country side, where he spent some time with them, and baptised", John 3:22. "The Pharisees heard that Jesus was gaining and baptising more disciples than John, although in fact it was not Jesus who baptised but his disciples", John 4:1-2.

Jesus Taught Baptism or Commanded It

"Then Jesus came to them and said, 'All authority in heaven and on earth has been given to me. Therefore go and make disciples of all nations, baptising them in the name of the Father and of the Son and of the Holy Spirit, and teaching them to obey everything I have commanded you. And surely I am with you always, to the very end of the age'", Matthew 28:18-20.

Eligibility for Baptism

The two-fold condition for baptism: The New Testament reveals that only born-again believers who had received a genuine experience from God, of the assurance of the forgiveness of their sins, and of their hearts cleansed by His precious blood. As such, baptism in water is for those who have fulfilled the two-fold condition of faith in Jesus and repentance of sins with a view to starting a new life in Christ. 1. Faith: "Whoever believes and is baptised will be saved", Mark 16:16a; 2. Repentance: "Repent and be baptised, every one of you, in the name of Jesus Christ for the forgiveness of your sins", Acts 2:38.

The Parent's Commitment to Their Children

At baby/child dedication, parents make a commitment before God and the church to bring up their children in the ways of the Lord, by instructing them in the Word of God and by modelling the Christian life to their children. This is a commitment and responsibility undertaken by the parents. When children become adults, the responsibility of the parents ceases, and God holds each one of these young adults personally responsible for his or her response to God, the responsibility of personal faith in the Lord and repentance of sins, and undertaking believer's baptism.

What Role Does Baptism Have in the Life of a Modern-Day Christian?

Water baptism celebrates that our past is separated from us through baptism. Our past is not only dead but also buried. We live separated from our past. It is through baptism that we celebrate being delivered from old, sinful habits, for which the blood has paid the price to set us free. We need to understand that it is on the merit of Christ's blood alone that our sins are forgiven. The blood redeems us from the penalty of sin. The water acknowledges our deliverance from the old life. Baptism is, therefore, extremely significant in the life of a believer:

1. Our obedience to Jesus Christ

The One to whom we have given our lives is Jesus Christ the Lord. Each name is significant. Jesus is the Saviour, because He died for us. Christ is the Living One, who has come to live in us. He is Lord, which means that He is owner, master and king. If He is our owner, we are His personal and precious possession. If He is our king, we should be His loyal subject. The One who died for us, and lives in us, should rightly rule over us. The whole question of our obedience to Jesus Christ is really a test of our love for Him and our trust in Him. Jesus said, "If you love me, you will obey what I command", John 14:15. Jesus also said, "You are my friends if you do what I command", John 15:14. Jesus Christ is the living, risen Lord, whose life has the power to change a dying world. He commanded his followers to preach the good news about Jesus to the world and make disciples, or other followers of Jesus (Matthew 28:19-20). The way this is to be done is two-fold: by 'baptising them' ... and by 'teaching them to obey everything I have commanded you.' Peter did just this when he commanded those who heard his message to be baptised: "Repent and be baptised...", Acts 2:38.

2. Our identification with Him

When we are baptised we identify with His death and burial. Baptism is a death certificate administered. It basically is a public statement that the Christian's old life and past deeds have been put to death in Christ and buried with Him. In baptism we also identify with His resurrection. Baptism for the Christian is, in truth, is not only a dying but also a rising again to a new life, because we believe that Christ had died and risen again and that we share in this experience of our Lord. It becomes real in our experience as we believe intensely in and identify with the life and death and resurrection of Jesus Christ. We read in Romans, "All of us who were baptised into Christ Jesus were baptised into his death. We therefore buried with him through baptism into death in order that, just as Christ was raised from the dead through the glory of the Father, we too may live a new life", 6:3-4. Paul sums up the Christian message by linking these together. "Christ died for our sins....He was buried.... He was raised on the third day...," 1 Corinthians 15:3-4.

3. Jesus Christ sanctifies us

Water baptism teaches the believer that he is sanctified. This simply means he is separated from his past sin and old life and set apart to God. This is summed up by these two expressions: "Count yourself dead to sin and alive to God in Christ Jesus", Romans 6:11; and "Therefore, if anyone is in Christ, he is a new creation; the old has gone, the new has come!", 2 Corinthians 5:17. Can you imagine how powerful baptism becomes in the life of new believers who have realised that their old life with its habits, addictions, or whatever has haunted or oppressed them, has now been buried through their identification with Christ in baptism. This great truth is clearly demonstrated as we are baptised by full immersion into water.

Practice of Baptism

Baptism in the time of Apostle Paul was three things. It was adult baptism; it was instructed baptism; it was baptism by total immersion. Therefore the symbolism of baptism was clear as the waters closed over the head of the one being baptised, it was as if the individual died; rising up again from the water, it was as if the individual rose to new life. The old life is now dead and buried; a new individual has risen to a new life. Baptism is carried out by authorised believers for the new believer as soon as they are ready after becoming Christian. The new believer would give public testimony to their faith in Jesus, and those baptising would affirm their commitment by saying, 'Upon the confession of your faith in the Lord Jesus Christ, the Son of God, and by His authority, I baptise you "in the name of the Father, and of the Son and of the Holy Spirit"', Matthew 28:19.

Why Baptism Is Important

The importance of baptism can be best summarised by the statement made by Paul Koshy, "When Jesus calls us into a lifelong relationship of following him, the first thing he calls us to is to be baptised in water. Baptism is a response to Jesus and his words, and it is part of his provision for our lives. Baptism presses closer into Jesus as we obey him and as we identify with his death in our place, his burial and his resurrection from the dead. In it, we are making a clear break from our old way of life and embracing the new life that comes from a personal relationship with Jesus. Baptism is that decisive, public and exclusive step of commitment that launches us forward into a life of following Jesus and sharing in his mission to rescue the world"[1].

Concluding Remarks

Through baptism we respond in obedience, demonstrating to our family and the world the meaning of our faith in Christ, the only one who is able to change us. Eternal life is God's life embodied in Christ given to all believers now as a guarantee that they will live forever. In eternal life there is no death, sickness, oppression, evil or sin. If we want to follow Christ we must "repent and be baptised", Acts 2:38. We must turn to Christ, depending on Him for forgiveness, mercy, guidance and purpose. Baptism identifies us with Christ and with the community of believers. Baptism parallels the death, burial, and resurrection of Christ, and it also portrays the death and burial of our sinful old way of life followed by resurrection to new life in Christ. It is a condition of discipleship and a sign of faith. Baptism is a tremendous blessing and a great moment in a Christian's life.

Receiving Jesus as the Lord of our lives is the beginning of a life with Him. We have studied together the Biblical foundation of baptism. In the next chapter we will look at God's provision of power to live the Christian life.

Chapter 3

GOD'S POWER FOR LIVING – THE HOLY SPIRIT

*Don't you know that you yourselves are God's temple and
that God's Spirit lives in you?* (1 Corinthians 3:16)

Introduction

Many of us are familiar with the blessing or benediction said by the
priest or an elder at the conclusion of a church service or a prayer
meeting, 'In the name of the Father, the Son and the Holy Spirit' or
"May the grace of the Lord Jesus Christ, and the love of God, and
the fellowship of the Holy Spirit", 2 Corinthians 13:14. The Bible
describes a triune God – God the Father, God the Son and God the
Holy Spirit. But sadly, most of us have very limited understanding
or experience of the Holy Spirit and acknowledge the Holy Spirit
minimally in our day-to-day lives. The presence of the Holy Spirit
is the greatest and the best asset any believer can have. Therefore, let
us prayerfully study together the awesome topic of the baptism in
the Holy Spirit, with a desire to know the person of the Holy Spirit
in a greater way and to experience more of His presence in our lives.

Who Is the Holy Spirit?

The Holy Spirit is God; He is one with, yet distinct from, the Father and the Son. He is the third person of the godhead. The Holy Spirit is spoken of right from the beginning of the Bible as the 'Spirit of God'. Genesis 1:2 tells us that at the very moment of creation, "...the Spirit of God was hovering over the waters." In the Old Testament we see that the Holy Spirit came upon certain people at certain times, in order to enable them to speak to people on behalf of God and perform some mighty acts. In the New Testament the Holy Spirit is made available to everyone who is born again. The Holy Spirit is a person, and He has a personality just like God the Father and God the Son. He knows things, exercises His will, feels, speaks, leads and teaches (1 Corinthians 2:10-11, 12:11; Acts 13:2; Luke 4:1; John 14:26), and when we sin, we quench or grieve the Holy Spirit: "And do not grieve the Holy Spirit of God, with whom you were sealed for the day of redemption", Ephesians 4:30.

The Holy Spirit Possesses the Divine Attributes of the Godhead:

1. *He is a Person:* "But when he, the Spirit of truth, comes, he will guide you into all   truth. He will not speak on his own; he will speak only what he hears, and he will tell you what is yet to come. He brings glory to me by taking from what is mine and making it known to you", John 16:13-14. "While they were worshiping the Lord and fasting, the Holy Spirit said, 'Set apart for me Barnabas and Saul for the work to which I have called them'", Acts 13:2.

2. *He is equal with God the Father and God the Son:* "For prophecy never had its origin in the will of man, but men spoke from God as they were carried along by the Holy Spirit", 2 Peter 1:21. "Then

Peter said, 'Ananias, how is it that Satan has so filled your heart that you have lied to the Holy Spirit and have kept for yourself some of the money you received for the land? …What made you think of doing such a thing? You have not lied to men but to God'", Acts 5:3-4.

3. *He is the Creator, along with God the Father and God the Son:* "Then God said, 'Let us make man in our image, in our likeness…'", Genesis 1:26. "The Spirit of God has made me; the breath of the Almighty gives me life", Job 33:4.

4. *He is Omnipotent (all powerful):* "The Holy Spirit will come upon you and the power of the Most High will overshadow you", Luke 1:35a. "…by the power of signs and miracles, through the power of the Spirit…", Romans 15:19a.

5. *He is Omnipresent (present everywhere):* "Where can I go from your Spirit? Where can I flee from your presence? If I go up to the heavens, you are there; if I make my bed in the depths, you are there", Psalm 139:7-8.

6. *He is Omniscient (all knowing):* "…but God has revealed it to us by his Spirit. The Spirit searches all things, even the deep things of God", 1 Corinthians 2:10. "But when he, the Spirit of truth, comes, he will guide you into all truth", John 16:13.

7. *He is eternal:* "…who through the eternal Spirit offered himself unblemished to God…", Hebrews 9:14.

8. *He is imparts God's wisdom and power:* "The Spirit of the LORD will rest on him – the Spirit of wisdom and of understanding, the

Spirit of counsel and of power, the Spirit of knowledge and of the fear of the LORD – and he will delight in the fear of the LORD", Isaiah 11:2. "…how God anointed Jesus of Nazareth with the Holy Spirit and power, and how he went around doing good and healing all who were under the power of the devil, because God was with him", Acts 10:38.

The Ministry of the Holy Spirit

The Holy Spirit is the *Parakletos* – the comforter, intercessor, counsellor, helper. In John 14:16 Jesus said, "And I will ask the Father, and He will give you another Counsellor to be with you forever." The word translated 'counsellor' is translated from the Greek word *parakletos*, which means 'one who helps, by consoling, encouraging, or mediating on behalf of.' It is a rich word that can be translated 'counsellor', 'helper', 'comforter', 'encourager', 'intercessor' or 'mediator', and in the New Testament this word is used exclusively to refer to the Holy Spirit and to Jesus. In John 16:7, Jesus said, that it was better for us that He returned to the Father in order to send the Holy Spirit to us: "But I tell you the truth: It is for your good that I am going away. Unless I go away, the Counsellor will not come to you; but if I go, I will send him to you." The Holy Spirit is here on earth with us to help us in every situation.

The Holy Spirit is God's seal – His guarantee. We can see from the Bible that it was always God's plan to fill people with His Spirit (Joel 2:28,29 and Acts 2:17,18). The Holy Spirit's presence in our lives is described as a guarantee (assurance, pledge, promise, warranty) or a seal that proves that we belong to God. Paul wrote to the Ephesians, "Having believed, you were marked in Him with a seal, the promised Holy Spirit, who is a deposit guaranteeing our inheritance until the redemption of those who are God's possession – to the praise of His glory", Ephesians 1:13-14.

The Holy Spirit is the Spirit of truth—In John 16:13, Jesus said, "But when the Spirit of truth comes, he will guide you into all truth." The Holy Spirit guides into all truth by testifying to Jesus, who is the Truth, and by giving understanding and revelation of God's Word (John 15:26,14:26). The Holy Spirit brings glory to Jesus. "He will not speak on his own; he will speak only what he hears, and he will tell you what is yet to come. He will bring glory to me by taking from what is mine and making it known to you", John 16:13-15.

The Holy Spirit is the author and interpreter of the Scriptures – "All Scripture is God-breathed and is useful for teaching, rebuking, correcting and training in righteousness", 2 Timothy 3:16. "For prophecy never had its origin in the will of man, but men spoke from God as they were carried along by the Holy Spirit", 2 Peter 1:21. God gives us the Holy Spirit so that we can understand the Bible. In John 14:26, Jesus said, "But the Counsellor, the Holy Spirit, whom the Father will send in my name, will teach you all things and will remind you of everything I have said to you". The Holy Spirit who inspired the writing of Scripture also interprets it.

Holy Spirit bears witness to the truth about Jesus Christ – "When the Counsellor comes whom I will send to you from the Father, the Spirit of truth who goes out from the Father, he will testify about me", John 15:26. "We are witness of these things, and so is the Holy Spirit, whom God has given to those who obey him", Acts 5:32.

Holy Spirit convicts the world of sin – "When he comes, He will convict the world of guilt in regard to sin and righteousness and judgement: in regard to sin, because men do not believe in me; in regard to righteousness, because I am going to the Father, where you can see me no longer; and in regard to judgement, because the prince of this world now stands condemned", John 16:8-11.

Holy Spirit appoints and directs His ministers to places as He wills– "While they were worshiping the Lord and fasting, the Holy Spirit said, 'Set apart for me Barnabas and Saul for the work to which I have called them'", Acts 13:2. "Keep watch over yourselves and all the flock of which the Holy Spirit has made you overseers. Be shepherds of the church of God, which he bought with his own blood", Acts 20:28.

The Holy Spirit's Role in the Life of a Believer

The Holy Spirit testifies with our spirit that we are children of God (Romans 8:16);

The Holy Spirit makes known the love of God to our hearts, and gives us the power to love both God and people (Romans 5:5);

The Holy Spirit sanctifies us – sets us apart for God (Ephesians 1:13-14; Romans 15:16);

The Holy Spirit helps us to worship God in the Spirit (John 4:24);

The Holy Spirit helps us in prayer (Romans 8:26; Jude:20);

The Holy Spirit helps us to know God better (Ephesians 1:17);

The Holy Spirit enables us to bring forth the fruit of the Spirit, the character of Jesus (Galatians 5:22-23);

The Holy Spirit strengthens our inner being (Ephesians 3:16; Colossians 1:11);

The Holy Spirit gives life to our mortal bodies (Romans 8:11);

Holy Spirit leads and guides us (Romans 8:14; Acts 8:29);

The Holy Spirit grants power to be witnesses of Jesus Christ (Acts 1:8);

The Holy Spirit gives us supernatural gifts to use in his service (1 Corinthians 12).

The Teaching about the Holy Spirit in the Gospel of John

The incoming Spirit: "Jesus answered, 'I tell you the truth, unless a man is born of water and the spirit, he cannot enter the kingdom of God'", John 3:5. This is the commencement of the Christian life, the new birth by the Spirit. We are born by the Spirit into the family of God.

The indwelling Spirit: "But whoever drinks the water I give him never thirst. Indeed, the water I give him will become in him a spring of water welling up to eternal life", John 4:14. He fills us with His presence and brings us joy.

The overflowing Spirit: "Whoever believes in me, as the Scripture has said, Streams of living water will flow from within him. By this he meant the Spirit, whom those who believed in him were later to receive", John 7:38-39. Out of his inmost being shall flow rivers of living water – not just little streams of blessing, but rivers. For this to happen as Jesus said," if anyone is thirsty, let him come to me and drink", John 7:37.

The witnessing Spirit (chapters 14-16): Holy Spirit speaks through us. This is the particular task of the Christian – to testify of Christ through the enabling of the Holy Spirit. To try and live the Christian life without the Holy Spirit is like trying to drive a car without any fuel in the tank. God gives us the Holy Spirit so that we can be bold in our witness as Christians.

Baptism in the Holy Spirit – Being Filled with the Holy Spirit

When we go through the new birth, our spirit is transformed by the Spirit of God. "The old has gone and the new has come", 2 Corinthians 5:17. At this point we receive the Holy Spirit as a part of being connected to God. However, Jesus wants us to have the fullness of the Holy Spirit or the baptism in the Holy Spirit. Luke's record in Acts 1:4-5 tells us "…he [Jesus] gave them [his disciples] this command; Do not leave Jerusalem, but wait for the gift my Father promised, which you have heard me speak about. For John baptised you with water, but in a few days you will be baptised with the Holy Spirit." In Acts 2:4 we read, "All of them were filled with the Holy Spirit and began to speak in other tongues as the Spirit enabled them." When we read chapter one it is very clear that it was not just the apostles who were filled with the Holy Spirit but all who were gathered together, both men and women – about one hundred and twenty in all.

In Acts 2:4, when disciples received the baptism in the Holy Spirit, we see that they began to speak in other tongues, i.e. languages other than their own. In Acts chapters 10 and 19, when new believers were filled with Holy Spirit they too started to speak in tongues. Even today the infilling of the Holy Spirit, along with speaking in tongues, is for all who trust in Jesus. As Peter instructed his hearers in Acts 2:38-39, "Repent and be baptized, every one of you, in the name of Jesus Christ for the forgiveness of your sins. And you will receive the gift of the Holy Spirit. The promise is for you and your children and for all who are far off—for all whom the Lord our God will call."

Dear friends, don't think that the baptism in the Holy Spirit was a one off experience, only for that day of Pentecost. In Acts chapter eight we see that eight years after the day of Pentecost, while Philip was carrying the gospel to Samaria, signs and wonders took place. Although they had believed and been baptised in water, they had not yet been filled with the Holy Spirit. So when Peter and John went down to Samaria, they placed hands on them and prayed for them, and they received the Holy Spirit (Acts 8:14-17). Similarly we read in Acts 19, about twenty years after the day of Pentecost, Paul journeyed to Ephesus. Having recognised that they have not yet received the Holy Spirit, "Paul placed hands on them, the Holy Spirit came on them and they spoke in tongues and prophesied", Acts 19:1, 6.

The phrase 'speak in tongues' refers to the enabling of the Holy Spirit to speak in a language we have never learned. We sometimes feel limited by our own language and power of expression to communicate what we really feel in our heart and spirit. Speaking in tongues is a wonderful gift from our loving heavenly Father, which helps us greatly in expressing ourselves to God in praise, worship, prayer and intercession. Speaking in tongue helps us in praying under pressure or at other times when we don't know what to pray in our own language. Speaking in tongues is a gift that grows the more we use it – so persevere in using what God gives you, as it is a great gift to use and to develop.

Further Explanation of the Baptism in the Holy Spirit

The Greek word *baptizo*, from which we get the word baptism, means to dip or immerse. When a believer is baptised in the Holy Spirit, he is immersed in the Holy Spirit. At the same time he is 'filled with the Holy Spirit' (Acts 2:4). He is wrapped with the Holy Spirit within and without. It is like a sponge being immersed in water and water permeating the sponge. One is immersed in the Holy Spirit, while the Holy Spirit fills him to overflowing with His power and divine energy to live the Christian life. This overflowing experience is compared to rivers of living water, springing up and overflowing from our heart. "On the last and greatest day of the Feast, Jesus stood and said in a loud voice, 'If anyone is thirsty, let him come to me and drink. Whoever believes in me, as the Scripture has said, streams of living water will flow from within him'. By this he meant the Spirit, whom those who believed in him were later to receive", John 7:37-39a. This is just what happened on the day of Pentecost.

How Do We Receive the Baptism in the Holy Spirit

The Bible tells us in Luke 11:9-13 that by asking God, He will give us the Holy Spirit. As He fills us with the Holy Spirit, our part is that we should begin to speak out the words the Holy Spirit gives us. In Acts 19 we see that Paul placed hands on the believers and they were filled with the Holy Spirit. The Holy Spirit gives us power and enables us to do what He commands us to do. Jesus said, "Go into all the world and preach the good news to all creation...they will place their hands on the sick people and they will get well", Mark 16:15-18.

Being filled with the Holy Spirit is not one off thing. We see in Acts 4 that the same apostles, who had first been baptised in the Holy Spirit in Acts 2, were again filled with the Holy Spirit. Furthermore, when Paul says to the Ephesians (5:18), "Be filled with the Holy Spirit", he is encouraging the believers to go on being filled with the Holy Spirit.

The most common hindrances to be filled with the Holy Spirit can be doubt, fear or even feeling of inadequacy. As such, it is good to remember that: a) Our heavenly Father has promised to give the Holy Spirit to those who ask – and He always keeps His promises (Luke 11:9-13); b) Our heavenly Father, who is perfect, only gives good gifts to his children – and His best gift, along with giving His Son, is to give us the Holy Spirit (Matthew 7:7-11; Acts 1:4-8; James 1:17); and c) It is by faith – by trusting in Him, not by our works – that we receive the Holy Spirit (Galatians 3:14).

We need to do a number of things in order to receive this blessing

Be born again: The person who is going to be filled with the Spirit must first have turned to Jesus in repentance and faith (Acts 2:38). Surrender to God and be willing to obey Him (Acts 5:32).

Have a thirst and desire for the Holy Spirit: The Holy Spirit is God, and it is a privilege to receive Him. Jesus said, "If anyone is thirsty, let him come to me and drink" (v 37). Whoever believes in me, as the Scripture has said, streams of living water will flow from within him." (John 7:37-38).

Believe: The Bible says that it is by faith that we receive the Holy Spirit (Galatians 3:14). That means that we are trusting in Jesus that He has made us worthy to receive the Holy Spirit. Just as we could never earn our salvation, we cannot earn the baptism in the Holy Spirit. Just as we received our salvation by trusting in Jesus to take away our sins and give us a new life, so we trust Jesus to fill us with the Holy Spirit.

Ask God to be filled with His Spirit: Ask God for what He has promised. The Bible says, if we ask for the Holy Spirit, that prayer will be answered (Luke 11:9-13).

Receive the Holy Spirit: Thanksgiving is great 'receiver'. When someone we trust says that they will give us something, it is natural for us to thank them for it. Once we have asked God to baptise us in the Holy Spirit, we can begin to thank Him that He is doing exactly what He promised and then wait on Him and receive from Him with a worshipful heart as He fills us.

Start speaking in tongues: Open your mouth and start to praise God in the new language that the Holy Spirit gives to you. Believe that what you received is from God, persevere with it and see it grow. Acts 2:4 tells us that, "All of them were filled with the Holy Spirit and began to speak in other tongues as the Spirit enabled them." The Holy Spirit filled them and enabled them to speak in tongues, but they did the speaking. Similarly, as the Holy Spirit fills us, we need to open our mouth and speak.

It is worth noting that with our natural language, the words come from our mind to our mouth. However, the Holy Spirit does not fill our mind, He fills our innermost being, our heart. So in the case of tongues, the words come from our heart to our mouth. These are new words, words from the Holy Spirit, which our mind will not comprehend – that is normal. But we can ask God for the interpretation of those words, and also as we switch between tongues and our natural language we will find that speaking in tongues will result in us having greater expression in prayer and worship in our natural language, as without realising it we start to tune into what the Holy Spirit is saying through us.

Concluding Remarks

The Bible reveals the person of the Holy Spirit as been the primary agent involved in the ministry of the Word of God throughout the centuries. The Holy Spirit is revealed as a person, having the attributes of mind (Romans 8:27), will (1 Corinthians 12:11) and feeling (Ephesians 4:30). He can be lied to (Acts 5:3); He can be resisted (Acts 7:51); He can be blasphemed (Matthew 12:31-32); He can be quenched (2 Thessalonians 5:19). The Holy Spirit possesses the divine attributes of the godhead: He is eternal (Hebrews 9:14); omnipresent, omnipotent, and omniscient.

It is important for us to recognise the difference the Spirit makes to life. His presence in our lives is God's provision for us that enables us to live effectively. For this purpose, God promises the baptism in the Holy Spirit to all who trust in Jesus – we only need to thirst, reach out, ask Him and receive, and then enjoy the blessing. Being filled with the Spirit, however, is not a one-off experience, and it is essential that we learn to go on being filled with the Holy Spirit in order to continually embracing God's power for living.

As T. J. Bach said, "The Holy Spirit longs to reveal to you the deeper things of God. He longs to love through you. He longs to work through you. Through the blessed Holy Spirit you may have: strength for every day, wisdom for every problem, comfort in every sorrow, joy in His overflowing service"[1]. May we never cease to be grateful to God for the awesome privilege of being indwelt and empowered by the Holy Spirit. May we never put a limit on what the Holy Spirit in us is able to do both in and through our lives.

Chapter 4

THE GIFT OF GOD'S GRACE

In him we have redemption through his blood, the forgiveness of sins, in accordance with the riches of God's grace. (Ephesians 1:7)

Introduction

The grace of God is a soul-thrilling concept. The Bible reveals to us that the Lord is gracious; He is the giver of grace, He is the God of all grace and His throne is a throne of grace. The truth about God's grace must, therefore, be carefully guarded, passionately communicated, deeply appreciated and genuinely experienced. This chapter is an attempt to just do that – to communicate what God's grace is like, how it works in us, and how we can appropriate it.

Grace is a wonderful truth; it provides the basis for a right relationship with God. Through His redemptive work, Jesus made a way for us to know God as our Father, and this act of God's grace forms the fabric or substance of our relationship with God from beginning to end. Grace imparts divine life to us based on God's kindness for the purpose of making man a partaker of the divine nature and enabling the plan of God to be fulfilled through us. This truth is part of our daily walk in the Lord, in which God's grace is like a road for us to walk on from where we are to where God wants us to be.

I have heard a story that illustrates so well what grace is like: One day Abraham Lincoln watched a plantation owner bidding for a slave girl. Figuring he was going to buy her and abuse her, Lincoln paid the price to set her free. 'Does this mean, I can say whatever I want to say?' she asked. Lincoln replied, 'Yes.' Again she asked, 'Does this mean I can go wherever I want to go?' Again Lincoln responded, 'Yes, you're free!' With tears streaming down her face she replied, 'Then Sir, I will go with you.' What a lovely example of grace!

Grace Defined

Grace is God's unmerited spiritual favour and blessing; it is unearned and undeserved. In the New Testament, 'grace' (which is mentioned over 150 times) takes on a special redemptive sense in which God makes available His favour on behalf of sinners, who actually do not deserve it. Grace brings life and blessing to us from God. "Praise be to the God and Father of our Lord Jesus Christ, who has blessed us in heavenly realms with every spiritual blessing in Christ", Ephesians 1:3. It reveals God's love towards us. Romans 5:8 tells us, "But God demonstrates his own love for us in this: While we were still sinners, Christ died for us."

Grace is transforming; it is more than just an influence on man's thinking but rather it influences the heart of man. God spoke through Jeremiah, "I will put my law in their minds and write it on their hearts....I will remember their sins no more", 31:33-34. As

James Ryle put it, grace is 'the empowering presence of God that enables us to be who God has called us to be and do what God has called us to do'. Grace is the power of Christ's might transmitted to the believer! When Paul the apostle was under immense pressure through the persecution he faced continually, God said to him, "My grace is sufficient for you, for my power is made perfect in weakness", 2 Corinthians 12:9, and Paul's experience was that, even when he was weak in himself, 'Christ's power' rested on him through God's grace.

Two Biblical examples of God's grace

Ruth's story

In the book of Ruth, we see the providence of God at work in the life of Naomi, Ruth and Boaz. It is the story of God's grace in the midst of difficult circumstances. The book begins with funerals and ends with a wedding. Naomi moves from bitterness to blessedness, and Ruth moves from loneliness to love.

What a picture of the grace of God! Ruth was without a proper home, without adequate food and without a reliable companion, but she found a home in Bethlehem where she was loved and cared for by her kinsmen-redeemer, Boaz. In chapter one, Ruth had nothing but her faith (vv 16-17). In chapter two, she lived on leftovers (v 16). In chapter three, she received generous gifts (v 15). But in chapter 4, once she belonged to Boaz, everything he owned belonged to her (v 13). This story speaks to all of us, for we are all spiritually lonely, hungry and homeless until we are found by our Redeemer, Lord Jesus Christ. This is my story too!

Peter's story

Peter had been following Jesus for about three years when he hit the lowest point of his life. At the point when Jesus needed him the most, Peter had disowned or denied Jesus three times, (Luke 22:54-62). Having foreseen that this would happen, the Lord had prayed for him that, even though Peter himself would fail, his faith should not fail (Luke 22:31-34). The result was that Peter's faith was preserved, his relationship to the Lord was restored and he was re-commissioned to the work Jesus had called him to in a most profound fashion, (John 21:15-22). Just as Peter had denied Jesus three times, the Lord gave Peter the opportunity to reaffirm his – albeit imperfect – love for Jesus. Each time Peter stated his love for the Lord, Jesus gave him the charge to feed His sheep. Peter's restoration was truly of abounding grace.

Three Aspects of Grace

Grace is a spiritual substance, which we can and must receive and experience in increasing measure. God's provision of grace is sufficient for all our needs, but grace must be appropriated specifically from the Lord for the different areas of life – we need to receive grace upon grace. "For of His fullness we have all received, and grace upon grace. For the law was given through Moses, but grace and truth came through Jesus Christ", John 1:16-17, NASB. Just as different food groups are important for different aspects of physical development and functioning, grace profoundly affects different areas of our lives. As such, it is useful to consider and understand these major aspects of grace.

1. Saving grace

"For the grace of God that brings salvation has appeared to all men", Titus 2:11. Saving grace is God's power towards us resulting in our salvation. It transforms our heart, even instantaneously. It is by the grace of God we have been saved. "For it is by grace you have been saved, through faith – and this not from yourselves, it is the gift of God – not by works, so that no one can boast", Ephesians 2:8-9. Here, grace is described as the undeserved kindness by which salvation is given, but it is also a power-word describing the Holy Spirit's operational means. "Therefore, if anyone is in Christ, he is a new creation; old things have passed away, behold, all things have become new", 2 Corinthians 5:17. Amazing things happen when we call upon the name of the Lord; when we hear the good news about Jesus and we respond in faith, we access the power of God for salvation.

2. Standing grace

Once we have been saved, we are objects of God's grace. It is grace we are under and it is grace in which we now stand. "...since we have been justified through faith, we have peace with God through our Lord Jesus Christ, through whom we have gained access by faith into his grace in which now we stand", Romans 5:1-2. Standing grace is an ongoing impartation of God's power towards us that establishes and strengthens our hearts and causes us to stand in our day-to-day living for Jesus. However, we must actively access or receive it by faith. Standing grace benefits us personally and it causes us to live life out of God's strength rather than our own.

When I was incapacitated and confined to bed, a dazzling light came into my room. A voice said to me, 'you are blessed by My grace' (November 1991). His love, mercy and abounding grace have enabled me to rise from my sickbed, and empowered me to serve Him and minister to many since that time. Standing grace enables us to live victoriously in every circumstance.

Grace is multiplied primarily in the heart. If our heart is full of the things of the flesh, the enemy can easily influence us. So, it is important to guard our hearts with all diligence for it is the wellspring of life (Proverbs 4:13). 2 Peter 3:17 teaches us to avoid falling from steadfastness but grow in grace. Grace infuses our spirit with strength. "I can do all things through Christ who strengthens me", Philippians 4:13. In Ephesians 6:10, Paul says, "Finally be strong in the Lord and in his mighty power". Paul wrote to Timothy that, as no one stood up for him, he had to totally rely on God's strength to preach the gospel to the Gentiles (2 Timothy 4:16-17).

How can someone be strong in grace? It means trusting completely in Christ and His power and not trying to live for Christ in our strength to do His work. This grace strengthens us inwardly. Peter in his final greetings, he says, "this is the true grace of God, stand in it", 1 Peter 5:12. In grace we stand, out of grace we fall. Grace is linked by the knowledge of Jesus. Grace transforms our spirit with strength. Standing grace strengthens our heart and gives us the ability to stand in the midst of challenges and difficulties.

However, we need to exercise patience. Patience has an amazing quality that connects us from beginning to end. Paul says, "being strengthened with all power according to his glorious might so that you may have great endurance and patience" Colossians 1:11. "So do not throw away your confidence; it will be richly rewarded", Hebrews 10:35. God saw the end from the beginning when He promised Abraham his inheritance, and Moses the deliverance of His people from Egypt. Grace gives us strength to stand in that waiting time. What should we do during the waiting time? We continue to access grace through faith and receive strength to stand and we rejoice in the hope of the glory of God (Romans 5:2-3). Paul in his infirmities and in his weaknesses became strong in the grace of God (2 Corinthians 2:7-10). The way to stay in the will of God when circumstances are bad is by releasing faith through the mouth by praise. Grace changes us from the inside while faith moves circumstances. Even if the circumstance doesn't change, we still stand firm and learn to rejoice and glory in Him.

3. Serving grace

Serving grace is the unique empowerment, ability and divine equipment God gives to every believer according to the unique call and purpose of God for that individual. The apostle Peter said, "As each one has received gift, minister it to one another, as good stewards of the manifold grace of God", 1 Peter 4:4. The apostle Paul explained, "We have different gifts, according to the grace given us", Romans 12:6a. We are here on earth for a purpose; it is to take our place in the kingdom of God and to accomplish our God-given kingdom mission. We are to live a redemptive life and to manifest the heart of God to people who do not know Him yet.

Becoming a Christian means beginning a whole new relationship with God. We are no longer seeking to serve ourselves, but we are bearing fruit for God. Jesus said, "You did not choose me, but I chose you and appointed you to go and bear fruit – fruit that will last", John 15:16a. Paul wrote in Galatians 1:15-16, "But when God, who set me apart from birth and called me by his grace, was pleased to reveal his Son in me so that I might preach him among the Gentiles." Paul also declared, "By the grace of God I am what I am, and his grace to me was not without effect. No, I worked harder than all of them – yet not I, but the grace of God that was with me",1 Corinthians 15:10. God empowers people for His service when we are willing, and we each have a unique part to play in God's big plan of redemption. "By the grace God has given me, I laid a foundation as an expert builder, and someone else is building on it", 1 Corinthians 3:10.

Accessing God's Grace

Through faith – We access God's grace through faith – a response of trust in who He is and what He says to us. Faith, however, needs expression. Verbal confession declares, confirms and seals the faith that is in our hearts. "That if you confess with your mouth, 'Jesus is Lord,' and believe in your heart that God raised Him from the dead, you will be saved. For with your heart that you believe and are justified, and it is with your mouth that you confess and are saved", Romans 10:8-9. As we receive and respond to God's Word, the power of God transfers us from the kingdom of darkness into the kingdom of light, transforms our inner being and makes us a new creation. Thank God for His marvellous grace.

Faith is also expressed in action in response to God's Word. We only learn to trust God by doing it. We grow in grace by practising putting our trust in Him, counting on His grace provision for each day, and His intervention in situations that are difficult or impossible for us. Every day we need God's grace and, if we willingly acknowledge it and receive it by faith, there will be no shortage of it.

Through humility – Grace excludes merit. No one can earn God's grace by works of independent human effort, which result in pride. "And if by grace, then it is no longer by works; if it were, grace would no longer be grace", Romans 11:6. In fact, it is grace that teaches us to resist ungodliness and live righteously (Titus 2:12). God resists pride, which causes us to put dependency on ourselves and not on God. Rather we are to depend on God's kindness, placing our trust in Him, responding to Him and co-operating with Him. As James 4:6 tells us, "God opposes the proud but gives grace to the humble."

Through a growing relationship with Jesus – 2 Peter 1:2 NKJV tells us, "Grace and peace be multiplied in you in the knowledge of God and of Jesus our Lord". 2 Peter 3:18b instructs us to "grow in the grace and knowledge of our Lord and Saviour Jesus Christ." Grace is a gift from God, it comes through Jesus Christ and we grow in grace through our relationship with Him.

Through prayer – We also access grace in prayer. Jesus taught, "Pray that you may not enter into temptation", Luke 22:40-41. Jesus accessed strength in prayer and He was able to finish His purpose on earth. To the unsaved, God's throne is a throne of judgement (Revelation 20:11-15); but to God's children, it is a throne of grace. When we are tempted, we can come to our great High Priest for mercy and grace. "Let us then approach the throne of grace with confidence, so that we may receive mercy and find grace to help us in our time of need", Hebrews 4:16. If we sin we can come to our Advocate for forgiveness (1 John 1:9-2:2). We can come to Him anytime, every time and for any need, for the Bible categorically promises that He is able to save completely those who come to God through Jesus, because He ever lives to intercede on our behalf (Hebrews 7:25). The Bible also reveals that God is the One who "equips [us] with everything good for doing His will" (Hebrews 13:20-21).

Through living by the Holy Spirit – The Holy Spirit is "the Spirit of grace" (Hebrews 10:29), and God's grace comes to us through Jesus and by the Holy Spirit's presence and activity in our lives. Romans 8 tells us that: "through Christ Jesus the law of the Spirit of life set me free from the law of sin and death", (v 2); "the mind controlled by the Spirit is life and peace" (v 6); "if by the Spirit you put to death the misdeeds of the body, you will live" (v 13). When there is conflict between the flesh and the spirit, we need to learn to walk in the Spirit; the only way to overcome flesh is to stay in the Spirit. Jesus set an example for us. Jesus was friend of sinners, but kept Himself safe from sinning. He was here to give something to the world, not to receive from the world. God is jealous over our love and affection to the things of the world. He gives more grace than the pull of the world and temptation and pressure of the world.

Concluding Remarks

Grace is God's operational power for every aspect of life, whether for salvation, day-to-day living or service of God. Grace is a substance that flows to us out from our gracious God. Grace comes to us through His Son, the Lord Jesus Christ, and by the Holy Spirit's presence and activity in our lives. Grace is divine empowerment to do what is right, to stand and not fall. Grace can never be earned; it is a gift. There is only one channel of grace; it is solely through Jesus. Grace includes everything Jesus did for us in the atonement or reconciliation. Faith merely appropriates what God has already provided by grace.

Grace is a daily experience and must be embraced continuously. We can be daily strengthened in the inner man by the grace that is in Christ Jesus. Only God's grace can enable us to be who we were made to be, as it works in us and through us. Grace is multiplied in our lives us through a growing knowledge of our Lord Jesus Christ, and a vital relationship with Him. God's grace is accessed as we come humbly, yet boldly, before His throne of grace in prayer, and actively appropriate it by faith.

Chapter 5

THE JOY OF FORGIVENESS

Blessed is he whose transgressions are forgiven,
whose sins are covered. (Psalm 32:1)

Introduction

Forgiveness is one of the most wonderful words in the Bible. Without it, heaven's doors are closed. When Jesus uttered on the cross, "Father, forgive them, for they do not know what they are doing", Luke 23:34, this release of forgiveness brought sinners to heaven. Forgiveness turns darkness into light, confusion into peace, fear into faith, sadness into gladness, despair into hope, hatred into love, sickness into health, weakness into strength, a sinner into a saint and hell into heaven! Yes, it is like healing when we are sick, relief when we are burdened, and reconciliation when we have hurt someone (Psalm 32).

The Definition of Forgiveness

Forgiveness is an act of release, it is to show mercy and compassion to someone who has wronged us, it is a pardon for sins. However, true forgiveness is erasing every resenting thought or attitude, healing every hurt feeling and restoring a better and purer love for the offender. All of this is possible because of Jesus. When the Bible says, "The Word became flesh" (John 1:14a), it means that Jesus, the Son of God, became human; he became one of us. By doing so, Christ became a) the perfect teacher – by His life we see how God thinks and therefore how we should think (Philippians 2:5), b) the perfect example – as a model of what we are to become, He shows us how to live and gives us the power to live that way (1 Peter 2:21), c) the perfect sacrifice – Jesus came as a sacrifice for all sins, and His death satisfied God's requirements for the removal of sin (Colossians 1:19-23). This is the way our sins have been forgiven; Yes, Jesus paid the full price of our sin by His death. To pay the penalty for sin a life had to be given and God chose to provide the sacrifice Himself. The sins of the world were removed when Jesus died as a perfect sacrifice. We can receive forgiveness by confessing our sin to Him and asking for His forgiveness.

Gift of Forgiveness

There are numerous blessings contained in the gift of forgiveness. When we are forgiven by the Lord, we receive the riches of His grace along with it. "Praise be to the God and Father of our Lord Jesus Christ, who has blessed us in the heavenly realms with every spiritual blessing in Christ. ... In Him we have redemption through his blood, forgiveness of sins in accordance with riches of God's grace" Ephesians 1:3, 7.

The Power of Christ-like Forgiveness

It can heal broken hearts, broken lives, broken relationships, broken marriages and broken families. At the time Jesus prayed, 'Father, forgive them, what they do not know what they are doing', He was experiencing, a) a state of total humiliation b) the weakest point of His physical life c) the worst condition of suffering d) the most extreme pain, both physically and emotionally. But what was the outcome of that prayer? Today millions and millions are being forgiven and released from the power of eternal death and destruction. By learning to forgive we also can help release millions from the power of separation, sickness, death and destruction.

Forgiveness and love is first released from the heart by an act of decision; that is Christ-like forgiveness and it makes all the difference. By forgiving, we release both ourselves and others. Those who cannot forgive others wholeheartedly can never enjoy true freedom. Forgiving is often evidenced by going the extra mile. Personally, when faced with a situation where I was falsely accused, the choice left to me was to exercise the forgiving love and go on valuing that person as if nothing had ever taken place. It worked wonders! From that time on, our department became so peaceful.

To be free from our resentments, anger, fears, shame, bondage, spiritual death and sometimes sickness, we need to give and receive forgiveness in all areas of our lives. Often forgiveness is appreciated is a beautiful idea until we have to practise it.

Five Aspects of Forgiveness

1. Receive and accept God's forgiveness

The first and most important forgiveness is extended from God to us. By Jesus' death on the cross all our sins were cancelled – paid in full; a free gift for those who believe in Him as the true and highest authority, Saviour and Lord. Remember, if God was not willing to forgive sin, heaven would be empty. Jesus exclaimed from the cross, "It is finished", John 19:30. It means paid in full, and we need to accept Jesus' perfect sacrifice, his work on the cross on our behalf. The grace of God is always sufficient. His forgiveness is always complete. Forgiveness can then be extended from us to others.

Our God is a God who sees everything. We must be serious with our invisible sins, that is, those in our thoughts, imaginations, desires, and so on. Let us take time to examine our hearts and ask the Lord for forgiveness for all our sins, including the secret sins. God responds to our confession and repentance with complete forgiveness when we come to Him in earnestness. King David committed adultery with Bathsheba and murdered her husband to cover it up. But when David was truly sorry for what he had done and repented all those sins, God mercifully forgave him. No sin is too big to be forgiven, (see Psalms 51 and 32).

Confession and repentance

We need to recognise our sinfulness and tendency to do wrong; we need to realise that sin is rebellion against God Himself; we need to admit our sins to God; we need to trust in God's willingness to forgive, and we need to accept His forgiveness purchased for us through Jesus. God wants to forgive sinners. Forgiveness has always been part of His loving nature – God announced this to Moses (Exodus 34:7); He revealed it to David; and He dramatically showed it to the world through Jesus Christ. God longs to guide us with love and wisdom rather than punishment. He offers to teach us the best way to go (Psalm 32:7-8). Accept this invitation from God.

To confess our sin is to agree with God, acknowledging that He is right to declare that what we have done is sinful and that we are wrong to desire it or do it; it is to affirm our intention of abandoning that sin in order to follow Him more faithfully.

In Psalm 32, King David expresses the joy of forgiveness after he confessed his sin to God. We must ask God to cleanse us from within (Psalm 51:7), clearing our hearts and spirits for new thoughts and godly desires. God looks for a broken spirit and a contrite heart. Some of those who get irritated and angry with others (for example taking out their frustration on their children, wife, or husband etc), often have secret or un-confessed sins in their lives. If we do not experience this first step in Christian life, of receiving forgiveness from God, we may also fail to enter into the other four aspects of forgiveness.

2. Forgive others who have hurt us

Until we are able to realise it and forgive it, it will continue to hold us prisoner. It is us who are hurt the most when we allow un-forgiveness a place in our lives. It is a terrible thing that some of you reading this have been the victims of violence, sexual abuse, physical abuse, emotional abuse or neglect. But you will not find peace and freedom from your perpetrator until you are able to forgive that person. Forgiveness enables us to be released from the power that this the person has had over us. It sets us free. This type of forgiveness is often a process.

Quite a number of well-meaning Christians are deceived into thinking that they have forgiven others, while the truth is otherwise. When we learn to forgive others wholeheartedly, we lay a strong foundation in our Christian life, ministry, family etc. If this blessed truth is properly grasped, Christian marriages, families and homes can virtually be heaven on earth!

The Bible says in Romans 12:17-18, "Do not repay anyone evil for evil. Be careful to do what is right in the eyes of everybody. If it is possible, as far as it depends on you, live at peace with everyone.

Do not take revenge, my friends, but leave room for God's wrath for it is written: 'it is mine to avenge; I will repay' says the Lord". May the Lord open our spiritual eyes to see the blessed truth of forgiving others from the heart.

3. Keeping a right attitude towards God

God is perfect in love, mercy and grace. He loved us so much that gave us a free will. He wanted us to love Him as our choice. The harm others did to us was from their free will. It was their choice; it was not God's will, and God did not do it. On 4th March 1991, almost twenty two years ago, I underwent a back operation. It proved to be totally unsuccessful, resulting in disability and constant pain, and meant that I had to give up a University Senior Lecturer post. This was not God's doing; it was the result of human error. The failure that occurred during surgery and in after care, I could not blame God for. I say that from conviction, because I know that God loves me so much that He gave His one and only Son to die for me as a substitute for my sins.

There are times when we human beings in our frailty, fail to understand the work of God (Romans 8:28). In our hearts, perhaps in our weakness and suffering, we question God, 'Lord, why did you take away my loved one?'; 'Why is this happening to my marriage?'; 'Why did you allow this sickness in my child's life?'; 'I always have this financial problem'. There may be literally hundreds of situations that we cannot understand. It is easy to develop a grudge in our hearts towards God, which can grow and swallow up what is good. It is true we do not understand many things that are happening in our lives. "The secret things belong to the LORD our God, but the things revealed belong to us...", Deuteronomy 29:29. God's promise, however, is that, "the God of all grace, who called you to his eternal glory in Christ, after you have suffered a little while, will himself restore you and make you strong, firm and steadfast", 1 Peter 5:10. Be patient – your God will come as He promised. "I will not forget you! See, I have engraved you on the palms of my hands…", Isaiah 49:15b-16a).

If we don't appreciate and believe the basic truth that 'God is good and He does good' (Psalm 119:68a) and that "Every good gift and every perfect gift is from above, and comes down from the Father of lights, with whom there is no variation or shadow of turning", James 1:17, NKJV, it could also be possible to develop a grudge in our heart towards God which will hinder our faith in God. In John 10:10 Jesus clearly states that it is the thief (Satan) that comes to "steal, kill and destroy, but that He has come to give us life and life more abundantly".

4. Ask forgiveness from others

Even if we have not done anything knowingly against anyone, if we know someone is hurt by us, we must seek to be reconciled with them. In Matthew 5:23-24 we read, "Therefore, if you are offering your gift at the altar and there remember that your brother has something against you, leave your gift there in front of the altar. First go and be reconciled to your brother; then come and offer your gift".

God is interested in how we treat one another, and in the condition of our horizontal relationships. Our closeness to Christ can be hindered, or we may lose the presence of God, if we not seeking to be at peace with others (Hebrews 12:14). Jesus said, "And when you stand praying, if you hold anything against anyone forgive him, so that your Father in heaven may forgive your sins", Mark 11:25-26. An unforgiving spirit conceives hatred and begets the spirit of murder. When we hate others, we will kill the peace, the joy, the grace and finally the eternal life that are meant to be ours in Christ Jesus (1 John 3:15).

It is essential to ask forgiveness from others as soon as we realise our mistakes. Very often, husband–wife relationships are strained because one or the other delays or refuses to ask forgiveness or issue forgiveness due to pride or stubbornness. In some cases, the husband may expect or demand forgiveness first from the wife or vice versa. The right spirit is to ask forgiveness from others, even if our mistake is very negligible. God holds us responsible for our part in the matter (Romans 12:18-20).

5. Forgive yourself

You may feel that the guilt and shame of the past is too much to forgive. But you need to forgive yourself. God says in Isaiah 1:18-19, "Come now let us reason together". "Though your sins are like scarlet, they shall be as white as snow; though they are red as crimson, they shall be like wool. If you are willing and obedient you will eat the best from the land." Remember, that because of Jesus, "there is no condemnation for those who are in Christ Jesus", Romans 8:1. Forgiveness is all about letting go. It is a decision of our heart; it is an act of will to forgive. Many children of God are living in a condemned state. Although God forgave their sins when they genuinely repented and confess them, they find it hard to forgive themselves.

The Word of God says, "For I will forgive their wickedness and will remember their sins no more", Hebrews 8:12. When we truly repent of our sins, our God not only forgives but also forgets. Let us, therefore, forgive ourselves because our God has forgiven our sins and forgotten them all. The apostle Paul said, "But one thing I do: Forgetting what is behind and straining towards what is ahead, I press on towards the goal to win the prize for which God has called me heavenwards in Christ Jesus", Philippians 3:13b-14.

The Importance of Forgiveness

The basis of forgiveness

The act of forgiveness has two parts. There is God's part, which is Divine. There is man's part, which is responding to the divine will of God. God's forgiving heart is well expressed in the Word of God: He's the God, "who forgives all your sins and heals all your diseases", Psalm 103:3; "You are forgiving and good, O Lord, abounding in love to all who call to you", Psalm 86:5; "If my people, who are called by my name, will humble themselves and pray and seek my face and turn from their wicked ways, then will I hear from heaven and will forgive their sin and will heal their land", 2 Chronicles 7:14; "If you, O Lord, kept a record of sins, O Lord, who could stand? But with you there is forgiveness; therefore you are feared", Psalm 130:3-4.

In the Lord's Prayer (Matthew 6:9-13), Jesus taught His disciples how to pray, "Forgive us our debts, as we also have forgiven our debtors" (v 12), followed by "...deliver us from the evil one" (v 13). There are two points to make here: a) Forgiveness is conditional (v 12, see also v 14-15) and b) Forgiveness is a legal requirement in order not to give a foothold to the devil to accuse us (v 13).

Our part in this is two-fold: Firstly, we are to receive forgiveness from God; Secondly, we are to forgive others as God has forgiven us in Christ Jesus, as explained above.

The significance of forgiveness

It makes salvation real: "...to give his people the knowledge of salvation through the forgiveness of their sins, because of the tender mercy of our God, by which the rising sun will come to us from

Examples of People Who Demonstrated Total Forgiveness

"I am your brother Joseph, the one you sold into Egypt! And now, do not be distressed...Joseph kissed all his brothers and wept over them. Afterwards his brothers talked with him", Genesis 45:4-5,15. Joseph's brothers, out of jealousy and malice, had sold him into slavery. But Joseph forgave his brothers of their wicked past, from his heart. As a result the relationship was restored. "But Joseph said to them, 'Don't be afraid. Am I in the place of God? You intended to harm me but God intended it for good to accomplish what is now being done, the saving of many lives. So then, don't be afraid. I will provide for you and your children.' And he reassured them and spoke kindly to them", Genesis 50:19-21. This passage highlights one example of true forgiveness.

Stephen's life and death is another prime example: "While they were stoning him Stephen prayed, 'Lord Jesus, receive my spirit.' Then he fell on his knees and cried out, 'Lord, do not hold this sin against them'", Acts 7:59-60.

Concluding Remarks

We have considered many aspects of forgiveness in this brief study. Let me now conclude by giving some practical tips:

Forgiving someone is an act of will and decision. Romans 5:5 tells us that 'the love of God has been poured out in our hearts by the Holy Spirit who has been given to us'. Therefore forgiveness has to do with a decision to obey God and yield to this love within. Negative emotions may still be there, but we have to remind ourselves that we have been forgiven the person. It is similar to when we first get saved – where we confess with our mouth the Lord Jesus and believe in our heart that God has raised him from the dead, then we receive salvation (Romans 10:9-10) This salvation is not based on 'feeling saved' but as an act of decision with our will. It is exactly the same with forgiveness. The Lord will help us and may give us practical things to do help our emotions come into line with our decision, for example, praying for the person, giving them a gift or by just reminding us how much He has freely given us.

May the Lord grant us the grace to live a transparent life, free from an unforgiving spirit and free from all un-confessed and un-forgiven sins. May God give us the grace to embrace the joy of forgiveness!

relationship. Jesus Christ "is the mediator of the new covenant", Hebrews 9:15, and "the covenant of which He [Jesus] is mediator is superior to the old one, and is founded on better promises", Hebrews 8:6.

Therefore, we see that the new covenant is a better covenant with better promises, and our mediator is the Lord Jesus Himself. We have a new and better basis on which to relate to God, with better promises. Jesus established the new covenant between God and us. Speaking of it, Jesus said these words in Luke 22:20, "This cup is the new covenant in my blood, which is poured out for you." Therefore, we see from the Bible that the covenant God made with us was a blood covenant – the strongest form of covenant.

Aspects of the Blood Covenant

A blood covenant is a binding, unbreakable agreement or contract made between two people or groups of people, established by the shedding of blood. All blood covenants have all or almost all of the following features: 1) It is established by the shedding of blood; 2) Blessings and curses, respectively, are pronounced for keeping and breaking the contract; 3) Gifts are exchanged; 4) Some form of eating or drinking; 5) A memorial is made. We can see these features in God's new covenant with us:

1. Established in Jesus' blood

Then He [Jesus] took the cup, gave thanks and offered it to them, saying, "Drink from it, all of you. This is my blood of the [new] covenant, which is poured out for many for the forgiveness of sins", Matthew 26:28. God's new covenant with us is established and sealed with the precious blood of His Son Jesus.

2. Blessings and curses

The old covenant that God established with the people of Israel contained many wonderful blessings for obedience to the Law, which was the terms of the old covenant, but also many terrible curses for disobedience. Jesus in His life on the earth perfectly fulfilled the Law, so that the blessings that God wanted to pour out through the old covenant could come to us in Christ in the new covenant. Furthermore, in His death on the cross He became a curse for us, in order to set us free from the curse of law. As Galatians 3:13-14 tells us, "Christ redeemed us from the curse of the law by becoming a curse for us, for it is written: 'Cursed is everyone who is hung on a tree.' He redeemed us in order that the blessing given to Abraham might come to the Gentiles through Christ Jesus, so that by faith we might receive the promise of the Spirit."

Let us also consider the following verses from the Bible:

Jesus said, "Do not think that I have come to abolish the Law or the Prophets; I have not come to abolish them but to fulfil them", Matthew 5:17. Paul said, "For what the law was powerless to do in that it was weakened by the sinful nature, God did by sending his own Son in the likeness of sinful man to be a sin offering. And so he condemned sin in sinful man, in order that the righteous requirements of the law might be fully met in us, who do not live according to the sinful nature but according to the Spirit", Romans 8:3-4. "He forgave us all our sins, having cancelled the written code, with its regulations, that was against us and that stood in opposed to us; he took it away, nailing it to the cross", Colossians 2:13-14. "For no matter how many promises God has made, they are 'Yes' in Christ. And so through him the 'Amen' is spoken by us to the glory of God", 2 Corinthians 2:20. "Praise be to the God and Father of our Lord Jesus Christ, who has blessed

"withhold no good thing from us who by faith are righteous with the righteousness of God in Christ Jesus."

"He [God] who did not spare his own Son, but gave him up for us all – how will he not also, along with him, graciously give us all things", Romans 8:32. God has already given us His very best in giving us his only begotten Son Jesus. So from God's part, He is not withholding anything from us. If we have the Son, then we also with Him have everything else as well. Our part is to receive it by faith, to take advantage of the benefits that have been purchased for us, to appropriate the blessings that have already been given.

In order for us to appropriate these covenant blessings, we have to know what they are from the Word of God and be fully persuaded that in the new covenant in Jesus' blood they are assured to us and we must be active in receiving them by faith. This is a faith that is: a) Fully persuaded in the heart; b) Speaks what it believes with the mouth (Romans 10:10); and, c) Acts in accordance with what it believes (James 2:14-26).

Our position with God is secured and assured by what Jesus has done for us, because of the covenant he has with us. However, it is important to note that we are called to a "faith expressing itself through love" (Galatians 5:6). We are called to live by the law of love. When we do not walk in love with others, then our faith is diminished, our prayers are hindered and as a result it is difficult for us to appropriate our covenant blessings.

It is also important for us to recognise that, not only does all that God has, belongs to us, but also all that we have belong to God. We have to be so persuaded in God as our covenant God – our covenant partner, who will never do us harm, but only good – that we will be prepared to do anything he says, go anywhere he says, etc. We belong to Him now. He is our God, and we are His people.

This exchange of possessions comes as a result of a change of identity that takes place in the new covenant. The old covenant dealt with external performance, but the new covenant starts with an internal transformation. "The time is coming," says the Lord, "when I will make a new covenant with the house of Israel... It will not be like the covenant I made with their forefathers when I took them out of Egypt...," declares the Lord. "This is the covenant that I will make with the house of Israel after that time," declares the Lord. "I will put my law in their minds and write it on their hearts. I will be their God and they will be my people", Jeremiah 31:31-33.

4. Change of name

Marriage is an example of the change of name and identity that results from entering into a covenant relationship. Following marriage a man becomes 'husband' and a woman becomes 'wife', and often the wife takes the husband's surname as her own. A change of name represents the fact that the two parties now identify themselves with each other. For example, Abram received a new name, Abraham, given to him by God; and the unchangeable God voluntarily also took on a new name and identified Himself as the God of Abraham.

For us in the new covenant, we take on the name of Christ – 'Christian', and we are now called children of God. On God's side, he now identifies himself as our Father, and we get to know Him in that way and call Him by that name.

In the beginning God delegated authority for the earth to mankind. When mankind sinned and rebelled against Him, God throughout history looked for and worked through covenant partners, by whom he gained access to the earth to influence its

the covenant blessings; b) Speaks what it believes; and c) Acts accordingly. It is a faith that expresses itself through love. It is a faith that perseveres until it inherits the promise. It is a faith that is also fully persuaded in the trustworthiness of God as our covenant God and partner, who can be entrusted with the whole of our lives.

We can have total confidence in our covenant relationship with God because it is based on Jesus' perfect life and has been established through Jesus' blood, and because God is a covenant-keeping God of commitment and total faithfulness.

Chapter 7

THE RIGHTEOUSNESS OF GOD

Blessed are those who hunger and thirst for righteousness,
For they shall be filled. (Matthew 5:6 NKJV)

Introduction

The subject of righteousness is perhaps one of the least understood doctrines of the Bible today. Yet, it is the very thing that God gave for men to have access to Him. God is righteous. Even though believers may not fully live in a way consistent with God's righteousness, God is perfectly righteous, and by His grace has forgiven us. Because of this great mercy from an all-righteous God, we should live a pattern of life consistent with God's own righteousness. The qualities of God are the attributes of God. His communicable attributes are love, justice, holiness, truth, mercy, wisdom and power. He alone possesses these qualities or attributes in perfection and perfect balance. Therefore only God is righteous. The rich young ruler came to Christ with a commendable record of law-keeping (Luke 18:18-23). Yet he obviously fell far short by his unwillingness to exchange his riches for the pre-eminence of God in his life. He therefore went sorrowfully away without the gift of eternal life. Because he lacked righteousness, the rich young ruler could not be accepted by the righteous God. True, he possessed some admirable qualities. But he did not possess all good qualities to perfection, and he did not possess them in perfect balance. It's imperative that we get back to the basics of righteousness. In this brief study, let us look at what the righteousness of God is, how righteousness is obtained and how sin affects a person's righteousness.

Righteousness Defined

A layman's definition of righteousness is simply, 'right standing with God'. Righteousness is the condition of being in right relationship with God. This can only happen through total faith and dependence upon Christ. There is no other way, and there is nothing we can add to our faith to obtain right relationship with the Lord. "And if by grace, then it is no longer of works; otherwise, grace is no longer grace" Romans 11:6 NKJV.

Gift of Righteousness

In the old covenant, righteousness had to be attained through keeping the law perfectly (Deuteronomy 6:25). It is the righteousness of man because it was to be attained through man's effort. It was the blood of animals that covered their sins till Christ came. To be righteous, God must keep all His attributes in perfect balance. Thus, God was faced with a problem. And it took the combined resources of the Trinity to solve that problem. Love found a way whereby God could retain His holiness, justice and truth, and yet show mercy. His wisdom designed that way. His power brought it forth to man. The incarnation (the taking by God of human characteristics in the person of Jesus) was the way. As love personified, God would so identify with man that His righteousness could be fully put to man's account. Man could thereby be called righteous. In the person of Jesus Christ, God came to man in complete and perfect identification. God is righteous so that man might have righteousness or be righteous, God gave Himself to man in the person of His Son. The Son of God became the Son of Man so that He might redeem the sons of men.

In the person of the Son of God, "Mercy and truth have met together; Righteousness and peace have kissed. Truth shall spring out of the earth, And righteousness shall look down from heaven", Psalm 85:10-11 NKJV. The first task for the righteousness of God, come to earth in the person of Christ was to atone for sin. This, Christ could do for He Himself was without sin. He that was without sin became sin for us, "that we might be made the righteousness of God in Him", 2 Corinthians 5:21 NKJV.

The only righteous person is the one with whom the righteous God has identified. Apart from this identification there is no righteous person. God has identified with man completely and perfectly in the person of Christ. It is upon this basis that the people of God bear the title, 'the Righteous'- a title previously belonging only to God. "This righteousness from God comes through faith in Jesus Christ to all who believe. There is no difference, for all have sinned and fall short of the glory of God, and are justified freely by his grace through the redemption that came by Christ Jesus", Romans 3:23-24. God does not simply 'declare' one righteous who is not. Declared righteousness is the result of the imputed (accredited) righteousness of Jesus Christ. The only true righteousness upon earth is imputed righteousness. One is righteous through the effectual grace which brings him into perfect identification with the righteous Son of God. It is upon the basis of this identification that one is declared righteous. He is righteous in Jesus Christ.

So, in the New Covenant righteousness is a gift (Romans 5:17; Ephesians 2:8). It is not something that we can earn. It is called the righteousness of God because Jesus kept the law and gave us His righteousness (Romans 10:3; Philippians 3:9). It is given by grace and received by faith. We as believers must understand that righteousness is a gift from God. Many Christians are still trying to attain righteousness through their own performance. Their sense of acceptance by God is based on their effort, but they always feel they don't measure up. They feel spiritually dry, burnt out and guilty with condemnation. We are members of His Body (1 Corinthians 12:13; John 15:1,5). God sees us 'in Christ' and has justified us forever. He sees us clothed in the righteous garments of Christ.

It Is All of God's Grace

Jesus saved the sinners by giving them grace. Through Jesus' death on the cross, His gift of righteousness has been imputed to all who believe in Him. When we understand that righteousness is a gift, we will have confidence because we know that it is based on His performance instead of ours. God loves us as much as He loves His own Son (John 17:23). He accepts us as He accepts Jesus Christ (Ephesians 1:6; 1 Peter 2:5). Therefore, we are eternally thankful because we received what we did not deserve. We live a life of worship and thanksgiving – singing of the amazing grace of our Saviour.

The Divine Exchange

Let us now go one step further in our understanding of righteousness. On the cross, there was a divine exchange between Jesus and man (Colossians 2:13-15). All our sins were imputed to Him to the extent that He became sin and all His righteousness was imputed to us to the extent that we became the righteousness of God in Christ. Jesus Christ is our Saviour, who obeyed God perfectly as our representative, and who died as our substitute sacrifice. Through Christ we have many blessings: reconciliation to God; righteousness and eternal life; identification with Him in His death, burial, and resurrection; being alive to God; freedom from condemnation; and an eternal inheritance.

The Just Live by Faith

The righteousness of God is God's way of justifying sinners, that is, putting them right with Himself without compromising His absolutely pure moral character. Habakkuk 2:4 indicates that salvation by faith alone was clearly taught in the Old Testament: "But the just shall live by his faith". The theme in Romans is 'the just' and how to be justified before God. Galatians 3:11 tells us how 'the just shall live' and the emphasis in Hebrews 10:38 on living 'by faith'. "For in it the righteousness of God is revealed from faith to faith; as it is written, 'The just shall live by faith'", Romans 1:17 NKJV.

Sin Consciousness

In the beginning when Adam sinned, sin entered the human race. Sin consciousness made Adam and Eve shy away from God and worked out their own solution by covering themselves with fig leaves. Sin consciousness makes us feel guilty and we can become striving to get back with God through our own effort. Sin consciousness is the basis of all religion trying to get back with God by work or human effort. But it does not work. Romans 5:12-21 teaches the imputing or charging of Adam's sin to the human race. Because Adam sinned as the head of the human race, all men are born into sin. We are possessed of Adam's nature (vv 12-14), and the sentence of death is imposed on us (Romans 6:23). The effect of Adam's fall is universal. Before receiving the gift if righteousness through the new birth, we were all fallen sons and daughters of old Adam. Before we are born-again, we did not become sinful by sinning; we sinned because we were sinful by nature. We sinned because we were sinners.

Righteousness Consciousness

The judgement of God rests upon all mankind outside of a saving relationship with Jesus Christ because of imputed sin, our inherited sin nature and our own personal sins. We stand guilty before God and deserve the death penalty until we come to Christ alone for a right standing before God (Romans 6:3). Moreover, in a similar way, the sin of man is imputed to Jesus Christ (2 Corinthians 5:21). Jehovah, the LORD God laid on his Son, the Lamb of God, the iniquities of us all (Isaiah 53:5; John 1:29; 1 Peter 2:24; 3:18). There was a transaction or the transfer of the sin of man to Jesus Christ, God's Sin-Bearer. The sin of man was imputed to Christ when He became the sin offering for the whole world.

When we are born-again we have become a new creation, created in Christ Jesus, made right with God. Paul the Apostle explains the mystery of righteousness that comes through faith in Jesus Christ – His life, death and resurrection. Paul says, "I have been crucified with Christ and I no longer live, but Christ lives in me. The life I live in the body, I live by faith in the Son of God, who loved me and gave himself for me", Galatians 2:20. When Christ died, Paul died; when He rose from the dead Paul also rose with Him. This means all believers can experience the resurrection life. Jesus said in John 15:4, "Remain in me, and I will remain in you". When we accept Jesus as our Lord and Saviour we are in Christ. When Jesus went to the cross, He took our sins and purchased forgiveness of sins for all those who believe. He took the punishment for our sins and declared us 'not guilty'. God sees us as He sees Jesus, righteous and holy. "We have been made holy through the sacrifice of the body of Jesus Christ once for all", Hebrews 10:10. "Now that faith has come, we are no longer under the supervision of the law", Galatians 3:25. Jesus' perfect life, His death on the cross and His resurrection enables us to have a relationship with God. "God made him who had no sin to be sin for us, so that in him we might become the righteousness of God", 2 Corinthians 5:21.

Standard of Righteousness

Jesus is our standard. God doesn't measure us against the standard of one another. The standard of righteousness is not about outward behaviour e.g. avoiding jewellery, the cutting or the growing of hair or such and dos and don'ts. If we don't believe and accept what Jesus did for us on our behalf, we can fall into the trap of religious rituals. God's righteousness is the standard by which everyone must be measured. We all must have a righteousness that exceeds anything we could ever produce through our own effort. That's where Jesus and His finished work on the cross comes in.

Concluding Remarks

Righteousness means having a right standing or right relationship with God who is holy and righteous. The Bible says, through Isaiah that our iniquities have separated us from God and our sins have hidden His face from us. It also tells us that, "all our righteous acts are like filthy rags", 64:6. In Romans Paul reminds us that there is no one that is righteous (3:10), not even one, all have sinned and fall short of the glory of God (3:23). But God in His unfailing love and mercy has made a way for us to have a right standing with God. In Romans 3:22, Paul states that this righteousness from God comes through faith in Jesus Christ to all who believe. Righteousness is a gift from God and we have to receive it by faith.

God sees us in Christ – and we are the righteousness of God in Christ. When we truly believe how our Father sees us, and when we start seeing ourselves in the same way, everything changes. Our faith is energised, we walk in the power of His Spirit, we have new desires from God, and we experience empowerment from Him.

The good news of Jesus Christ is more than a fact to be believed; it is also a life to be lived – a life of righteousness befitting the person "being justified freely by his grace through redemption that is in Christ Jesus", Romans 3:24 NKJV. God offers the gift of His righteousness to everyone who comes to Christ by faith. " 'Abraham believed God, and it was credited to him as righteousness'", and he was called God's friend", James 2:23.

Chapter 8

JESUS CHRIST, THE ONLY REDEEMER

...our great God and Saviour, Jesus Christ, who gave himself for us to redeem us from all wickedness and to purify for himself a people that are his very own, eager to do what is good. (Titus 2:13, 14)

Introduction

In the beginning, God created human beings after His own image, according to His foreordained plan in Christ that mankind should live holy and blameless before Him in love (Ephesians 1:4). However, since the rebellion of mankind against God, death came into the world and the whole creation was subjected to frustration and decay. In order that the whole creation be 'liberated from its bondage to decay', it was necessary that mankind first be redeemed to enjoy the glorious freedom of the sons of God (Romans 8:21-23). God now says, "Behold, I make all things new", Revelation 21:5 NKJV. This was possible only through the sacrifice, death and resurrection of our Lord Jesus Christ. Today, this glorious gospel of Jesus Christ is being proclaimed by His followers to the whole world for the redemption of mankind so that, in Christ, each person that responds to Jesus can be made a new creation (2 Corinthians 5:17).

The below are just a few of the many promises in the Word of God regarding the salvation He brings to people. God's plan is for people to be made perfect, just as Adam was perfect before his fall. Full provision for this to be found in Christ, the Lamb slain from the foundation of the world (Revelation 13:8). So, "...let us run with perseverance the race marked out for us. Let us fix our eyes on Jesus, the author and perfecter of our faith, who for the joy set before him endured the cross...", Hebrews 12:1-2; "It is because of him that you are in Christ Jesus, who has become for us wisdom from God – that is, our righteousness, holiness and redemption", 1 Corinthians 1:30. In this chapter, we shall study the five unique aspects of Jesus Christ whereby our salvation is complete and secure in Him and Him alone.

1. Christ's Offering of Himself As the Son of God

Christ, the second person of the Triune God, was willing to come down to the earth as "the last Adam" (1 Corinthians 15:45), to take the place of the first Adam, to rectify his faults and to restore to the human race all the blessings which they had forfeited by the fall of Adam. Christ was equal with God, sharing all the divine attributes of God the Father. He was willing to lay aside His divine powers and glory in order to come down and become a man; the most Perfect willingly became a substitute for the most imperfect and the vile, the Just for the unjust. "Very rarely will anyone die for a righteous man, though for a good man someone might possibly dare to die. But God demonstrates his own love for us in this: While we were still sinners, Christ died for us", Romans 5: 7-8. Furthermore, God rejoiced to accept Christ's decision to offer Himself totally for the redemption of humanity (Romans 3:24-25).

2. Christ's Spotless Life on Earth

When Christ laid aside His eternal glory and power and came down to dwell as an ordinary man, He lived spotlessly pure life, totally undefiled and perfect in every way, from the time of His conception to the day of His death on the cross. If Satan could have found the slightest taint of sin in Christ as a human being, He would no longer have been eligible as the Saviour of mankind. Praise God, His life as a man, lived within the limitations imposed upon every man, was without reproach. Jesus said, "I always do what pleases him", John 8:29b. Jesus asked, "Can any of you prove me guilty of sin?", John 8:46a.

It is worth mentioning the testimonies of those who knew Jesus when He was on earth, friend and foe alike bore witness to His sinlessness. Peter confirms that "He committed no sin", 1 Peter 2:22a; John testifies that "And in him is no sin", 1 John 3:5b; Judas cried, "I have betrayed an innocent blood", Matthew 27:4b; The Roman centurion said of Him, "Surely this was a righteous man", Luke 23:47b; Pilot himself confessed to the public, "I find no basis for a charge against him", John 18:38b. Jesus was the object of searching scrutiny for thirty-three and a half years by people from all walks of life. He emerges triumphant, His purity unsullied, His claims vindicated, His enemies silenced forever by His victorious shout: "I am the Living One; I was dead, and behold I am alive forever and ever! And I hold the keys of death and Hades", Revelation 1:18.

3. Christ's Death on the Cross

Christ's death on the cross brought a unique solution to the age-old problems of sin and death. Christ not only faced the problems of life on this earth with tremendous courage; He also willingly embraced a cruel and ignominious (public disgrace) death on the cross. Had He failed to do so, He would not have achieved His purpose for mankind; His indisputable divinity and His absolute holiness would not, of themselves, have brought about our redemption. Let us examine what Jesus accomplished through His death:

He took our sins upon Himself as a sin offering – "Look, the lamb of God who takes away the sin of the world!" John 1:29; "For Christ died for sins once for all, the righteous for the unrighteous to bring you to God. He was put to death in the body but made alive by the Spirit", 1 Peter 3:18; "But he was pierced for our transgressions, he was crushed for our iniquities; the punishment that brought us peace was upon him, and by his wounds we are healed. We all, like sheep, have gone astray, each of us has turned to his own way; and the LORD has laid on him the iniquity of us all", Isaiah 53:5-6.

He broke the power of sin – "For what the law was powerless to do in that it was weakened by the sinful nature, God did by sending his own Son in the likeness of sinful man to be a sin offering. And so he condemned sin in sinful man", Romans 8:3.

He took away our sicknesses and diseases – "...and he drove out the spirits with a word and healed all the sick. This was to fulfil what was spoken through the prophet Isaiah: 'He took up our infirmities and carried our diseases'", Matthew 8:16-17; "by his wounds you have been healed", 1 Peter 2:24b.

He has delivered us from the curse of the law – "Christ redeemed us from the curse of the law by becoming a curse for us, for it is written: 'curse is everyone who is hung on a tree'", Galatians 3:13.

He has delivered us from the present evil world – "...the Lord

Jesus Christ, who gave himself for our sins to rescue us from the present evil age, according to the will of our God and Father", (Galatians 1:3b-4).

He defeated the devil and his work in order to set us free – "Since the children have flesh and blood, he too shared in their humanity so that by his death he might destroy him who holds the power of death – that is, the devil– and free those who all their lives were held in slavery by the fear of death", Hebrews 2:14-15; "The reason the Son of God appeared was to destroy the devil's work",1 John 3:8b.

He made the way for us to be adopted as children of God – "But when the time had fully come, God sent his Son, born of a woman, born under law, to redeem those under law, that we might receive the full rights of sons", Galatians 4:4-5.

He has perfected us forever – "...by one sacrifice he has made perfect for ever those who are being made holy", Hebrews 10:14.

He has opened a new and living way into God's presence – "... we have confidence to enter the Most Holy Place by the blood of Jesus, by a new and living way opened for us through the curtain, that is, his body", Hebrews 10:19-20.

4. Christ's Blood

"To Jesus the mediator of a new covenant, and the sprinkled blood that speaks a better word than the blood of Abel", Hebrews 12:24. Through His blood, which was shed on the cross, Jesus has provided us with inexpressibly marvellous blessings:

Our life is atoned for – "it is the blood that makes atonement for one's life", Leviticus 17:11b.

We are redeemed – "In Him we have redemption through his

blood, the forgiveness of sins, in accordance with the riches of God's grace", Ephesians 1:7; "For you know that it was not with perishable things such as silver or gold that you were redeemed from the empty way of life…but with the precious blood of Christ, a lamb without blemish or defect", 1 Peter 1:18-19.

Our sins are forgiven – "This is my blood of the covenant, which is poured out for many for the forgiveness of sins", Matthew 26:28; "…without the shedding of blood there is no forgiveness", Hebrews 9:22.

We are cleansed from our sins – "…the blood of Jesus his Son purifies us from all sin", 1 John 1:7b.

We are justified – made right with God – and saved from His judgement – "Since we have now been justified by his blood, how much more shall we be saved from God's wrath through him!", Romans 5:9.

We are reconciled to God – "and through him to reconcile to himself all things, whether things on earth or things in heaven, by making peace through his blood, shed on the cross", Colossians 1:20.

Our conscience is cleansed so that we can serve God – "…the blood of Christ, who through the eternal Spirit offered himself unblemished to God, cleanse our consciences from acts that lead to death, so that we may serve the living God!", Hebrews 9:14.

We have access into God's holy presence – "…we have confidence to enter the Most Holy Place by the blood of Jesus…", Hebrews 10:19.

We overcome the devil – "They overcame him [the devil] by the blood of the Lamb…", Revelation 12:11.

5. Christ's Resurrection

A Christian's faith rests on the fact of Christ's resurrection. The cross without the resurrection has no power to change a person or impart life. But the fact is that Jesus Christ 'IS' risen from the dead, and the same power that raised Christ from the dead is able to supernaturally transform even the most depraved sinner and to bestow upon him eternal life.

The importance of the resurrection of Christ, with special reference to our redemption:

The resurrection of Jesus Christ is a fundamental truth in the teaching of the apostles – The resurrection of Jesus Christ is the backbone of the doctrines of the Body of Christ, the principal stone in the foundation of the church. It was the life and power of the witness of the disciples of Christ in the first century. "God has raised this Jesus to life, and we are all witnesses of the fact", Acts 2:32. The apostle Paul constantly exhorted the churches firmly to stand on the teachings of the resurrection of Jesus Christ (1 Corinthians 15:14,17).

The resurrection of Jesus Christ provides the sole authority for the Christian faith – Jesus' resurrection from the dead vindicates the Christian faith as nothing else could, and proves to His followers the validity of Christ's teachings and promises. "And if Christ has not been raised, your faith is futile…", 1 Corinthians 15:17.

The resurrection of Jesus Christ confirms the total cancelation of sin of those who trust in Him – "And if Christ has not been raised…you are still in your sins", 1 Corinthians 15:17; "For sin shall not be your master, because you are not under law but under grace", Romans 6:14; "When God raised up his servant, he sent him first to you to bless you by turning each of you from your wicked ways", Acts 3:26.

The resurrection of Jesus Christ confirms our victory over spiritual death caused by sin in the inner man – "For the wages of sin is death, but the gift of God is eternal life in Christ Jesus our Lord", Romans 6:23; "We were therefore buried with him through baptism into death in order that, just as Christ was raised from the dead through the glory of the Father, we too may live a new life", Romans 6:4.

The resurrection of Jesus Christ confirms the truth of the physical resurrection of the dead – "We believe that Jesus died and rose again and so we believe that God will bring with Jesus those who have fallen asleep in him", 1 Thessalonians 4:14; "because we know that the one who raised the Lord Jesus from the dead will also raise us with Jesus and present us with you in his presence", 2 Corinthians 4:14.

The resurrection of Jesus Christ confirms our justification before the throne of God – "He was delivered over to death for our sins and was raised to life for our justification", Romans 4:25.

The resurrection of Jesus Christ establishes our status as adopted sons of God, and as heirs with him – "Now if we are children, then we are heirs – heirs of God and co-heirs with Christ", Romans 8:17a.

The resurrection of Jesus Christ raises us up to higher spiritual plane – "And God raised us up with Christ and seated us with him in the heavenly realms in Christ Jesus", Ephesians 2:6; "… when he appears, we shall be like him, for we shall see him as he is. Everyone who has this hope in him purifies himself, just as he is pure", 1 John 3:2-3.

The resurrection of Jesus Christ, confirms the fact that he is able to complete his work in us, and to present us spotless before his throne – "To him who is able to keep you from falling and present you before his glorious presence without fault and with great joy – to the only God our Saviour be glory, majesty, power and authority, through Jesus Christ our Lord, before all ages, now and forever more! Amen", Jude 24-25.

The resurrection of Jesus Christ proves that He is God – "and who through the Spirit of holiness was declared with power to be the Son of God, by his resurrection from the dead: Jesus Christ our Lord", Romans 1:4. "Jesus said, 'Before Abraham was born, I am'", John 8:58; "that all may honour the Son just as they honour the Father. He who does not honour the Son does not honour the Father, who sent him", John 5:23.

The resurrection of Jesus Christ guarantees our salvation – "That if you confess with your mouth, 'Jesus is Lord' and believe in your heart that God raised him from the dead, you will be saved. For it is with your heart that you believe and are justified, and it is with your mouth that you confess and are saved", Romans 10:9-10.

The resurrection and ascension of Christ confirms Him as Head of the church, and as supreme authority over all principalities and powers – "For by him all things were created: things in heaven and on earth, visible and invisible, whether thrones or powers or rulers or authorities; all things were created by him and for him. He is before all things and in him all things hold together. And he is the head of the body, the church; he is the beginning and the firstborn from among the dead, so that in everything he might have supremacy", Colossians 1:16-18; "Therefore God exalted him to the highest place and gave him the name that is above every name, that at the name of Jesus every knee should bow, in heaven and on earth and under the earth, and every tongue confess that Jesus Christ is Lord, to the glory of God the Father", Philippians 2:9-11.

The resurrection of Jesus Christ establishes the reality of heaven, and of the certainty of the fulfilment of promises relating to eternal life – "Praise be to the God and Father of our Lord Jesus Christ! In his great mercy he has given us new birth into a living hope through the resurrection of Jesus Christ from the dead, and into an inheritance that can never perish, spoil or fade – kept in heaven for you", 1 Peter 1:3-4; (also see John 14:1-2).

The resurrection of Jesus Christ confirms the truth, His Second Coming – "In my Father's house are many rooms; if it were not so, I would have told you. I am going there to prepare a place for you. If I go and prepare a place for you, I will come back and take you to be with me that you also may be where I am", John 14:2-3; "…This same Jesus, who has been taken from you into heaven, will come back in the same way you have seen him go into heaven", Acts 1:11.

Concluding Remarks

The resurrection of Christ is the centre of the Christian faith and central fact of Christian history. Only Christianity has a God who became human, died for His people and was raised again in power. One central belief unites and inspires all true Christians – Jesus Christ is risen from the dead.

If Christ had not been resurrected from the dead, we could not be forgiven for our sins and we would have no hope of eternal life. Since Christ defeated death and conquered the grave as He promised, we know that what He said is true – He is God. Since Christ has been raised from the dead, we have certainty that our sins are forgiven. Since Christ lives forever to represent us to God – we are reconciled to God. Since Christ rose from the dead, we know we will also be raised.

Everyone in the world needs to be saved from the very nature of sin and reconciled to God, and this is possible only through Jesus. Our salvation, our justification and our cleansing comes as a result, not of our goodness or our worthiness, but of what Christ our Saviour, by His sacrifice at Calvary, has done for us.

Although God has finished the work of man's total salvation in and through Christ, we also have a response to make for this to be effective in our lives. Our part is to accept and appropriate this free salvation with true repentance, and fully surrender our lives into God's hands. It cannot be said too often that salvation is to be found in Christ and in Christ alone. "Salvation is found in no-one else, for there is no other name under heaven given to men by which we must be saved", Acts 4:12.

We want to honour all that Jesus has done for us on the cross, and to embrace the way of the cross for ourselves, while also knowing the power of His resurrection to set us free.

Chapter 9

JESUS CHRIST IS LORD

Therefore let all Israel be assured of this: God has made this Jesus, whom you crucified, both Lord and Christ. (Acts 2:36)

Introduction

The Bible's portraiture and revelation of Jesus Christ in all His glory and dignity is fascinating, enriching and life-giving. It reveals to us that Jesus truly is the answer to every human need. Only by being connected with Christ through faith can anyone enjoy a personal relationship with God and have power for living. Jesus is God incarnate and the only way to forgiveness and peace with God the Father. The whole account of Jesus' earthly life is contained in the four Gospels, each of which brings out a special emphasis. The Gospels present us with four portraits of Christ, the One who is himself the good news: Matthew – as Christ the King; Mark – Christ the Servant; Luke – Christ the Perfect Man; John – Christ the Son of God, emphasising his unique deity and essential humanity.

Who Is Jesus?

Bob Gass says, "He was born in the humblest of settings, yet heaven above was filled with the songs of angels. His birthplace was a cattle shed, yet a star brought the rich and noble from thousands of miles away to worship Him. His birth was contrary to the laws of life and His death was contrary to the laws of death, yet no miracle is greater than His birth, His life, His death, His resurrection and His teachings. He had no cornfields or fisheries, yet He spread a table for 5,000 and had bread and fish to spare. He never stood on expensive carpeting, yet He walked on the waters and they supported Him. His crucifixion was the crime of crimes, yet from God's perspective no less a price could have made possible our redemption. When He died, few mourned His passing, yet God hung a black cape over the sun. Those who crucified Him did not tremble at what they'd done, yet the earth shook under them. Sin never touched Him. Corruption could not get hold of His body. The soil that was reddened with His blood could not claim His dust. For over three years He preached the gospel. He wrote no book, He had no headquarters and He built no organisation. Yet 2,000 years later, He's the central figure of human history, the perpetual theme of all preaching, the pivot around which ages revolve, and the only redeemer of the human race....Let's join the wise men who 'fell down and worshipped Him' (Matthew 2:11, NKJV)"[1]. This gives us some insight into who Jesus is and what he has accomplished.

Jesus Christ is deity. He is the One who "was made flesh and dwelt among us", John 1:1. Jesus is the Son of God. He was God manifested in the flesh. He is the Way, the Truth, and the Life (John 14:6). He is alive today, and His name means everything.

Why Did Jesus Come?

Jesus came (among other reasons) to take dominion back from Satan and give it back to man, with Himself now the head of humanity. Jesus took by conquest all of the authority that Adam had forfeited to Satan in the Fall. Jesus, the Son of God, emptied Himself, was born of a human being and became a man so that He could conquer Satan as a man. In doing this, Jesus took back from Satan all the authority that had belonged to Adam (Colossians 2:15). All authority and power now belong to Jesus, which He exercises on earth through his church as we cooperate and participate in His ongoing plan of salvation today (Matthew 28:18-19; Ephesians 1:19-23). The power Satan uses in the earth now is illegitimate, and will one day be stripped from him when Jesus comes to judge the world.

Jesus, the Unique Child

Jesus was born in approximately 5 B.C. in Bethlehem, Israel, which was at that time occupied by the Roman Empire. Most people knew nothing about the birth of Jesus. The Bible tells us that Jesus was born of a virgin, named Mary, after the child had been miraculously conceived in her by the power of the Holy Spirit (Luke 1:26-35). His entry into this world was truly unique in character. The virgin birth emphasises that, although Christ is man, he is no ordinary man. He is the Son of God who has become the Son of Man; He is Immanuel – God with us! (Matthew 1:23).

Angelic visitations announced Jesus' birth to various people, and included remarkable statements about the person of Christ: "He will be great and will be called Son of the Most High" (Luke 1:32); "So the holy one to be born will be called the Son of God" (Luke 1:35). The Gospel of Luke tells how an angel appeared to some shepherds on the Judean hillside in the night to announce to them that a Saviour was born in Bethlehem, the city of David, and that they would find the baby laying in a manger. The angel said to them, 'Do not be afraid… Today in the town of David has been born to you; he is Christ the Lord'", Luke 2:10-11. After they had seen the Christ child, these shepherds ran to tell others what had happened.

Only Luke's gospel gives us a little insight into the childhood days of Jesus, telling us that He "grew and became strong, filled with wisdom; and the favour of God was upon him", Luke 2:40, 52. Even as a boy, Jesus longed to discern more of God's word and will. One time, at the end of a trip to Jerusalem, His parents discovered that they had lost Jesus, but 'after three days they found him in the temple courts, sitting among the teachers, listening to them and asking them questions.' In reply to His parents' anxious searching, Jesus replied, "Why were you searching for me… Didn't you know I had to be in my Father's house'", Luke 2:46, 49.

Many of the Jewish people of Jesus' day were awaiting the Christ (Messiah) whom they believed God would send to redeem the world from its fallen sinful state and bring in the kingdom of God. Just think, in Nazareth, where Jesus grew up, the members of the synagogue were attending services every Sabbath with the Redeemer, the Christ, and did not know it.

The Nature of Jesus

Jesus always stood out in a crowd, even in His humanity. He always attracted people to Himself. Mark tells us that the common people heard Him gladly (12:37). The needy sought Him out eagerly. Multitudes followed Him to hear His life-changing words. As "outstanding among the ten thousand" (Song of Songs 5:10), Jesus was quite conspicuous and distinguished. The Bible says in John

14:31, "but the world must learn that I love the Father and that I do exactly what my Father has commanded me..." Four traits, among many others, exemplified Jesus: Sacrifice (a sacrificial nature); Love (a motivating love); Obedience (an obedient will); and Courage (an unflinching courage). May it describe us as well as it does our Lord and Saviour.

Jesus' Ministry

The starting point for Jesus' ministry came when he was about thirty years old. Jesus was not a revolutionary political leader. He was no legalist. Jesus' reputation as a great teacher spread far and wide. He taught in parables, simple stories that made his lessons clear to all who were ready to learn. In the Sermon on the Mount, and on other occasions, he gave his hearers new insight into the nature of God, in how men should serve God and each other.

Part of the reason for his growing reputation was the miracles he performed. Jesus, the Son of God, identified Himself with us by becoming a man. He called Himself the Son of Man, and yet he unashamedly asserted, "I and the Father are one", John 10:30. Jesus' disciples slowly grew to realise the meaning of his claims. They walked with him and talked with him. They saw his miracles. They heard his teachings. One day, after Jesus had spent many months with his disciples, he asked, "Who do you say I am?", Matthew 16:15. Peter answered, "You are the Christ, the Son of the living God", Matthew 16:16.

The Lord's Supper

On the Passover evening, Jesus and his twelve disciples gathered to eat what was to be their last meal together. "While they were eating, Jesus took bread, gave thanks and broke it, and gave it to his disciples, saying, 'Take and eat; this is my body.' Then he took the cup, gave thanks and offered it to them, saying, 'Drink from it, all of you. This is my blood of the covenant, which is poured out for many for the forgiveness of sins'", Matthew 26:26-28. Following this Jesus went to the Garden of Gethsemane to pray. A mob sent by the chief priests and scribes, armed with clubs and swords and lead by the traitorous disciple Judas, entered the garden. Judas identified Jesus by greeting him with a kiss.

Jesus' Trial and Crucifixion

Jesus was tried, first by the high priest, Caiaphas, and then by Pontius Pilate, the Roman governor. Pilate was no personal enemy of Jesus and three times he tried to remove himself from the responsibility of passing a death sentence. He tried to pass the trial off to Herod, but Herod only sent Jesus back to Pilate. Pilate finally gave in to the pressure of Jesus' accusers. But he took water and washed his hands before the multitude, saying, "I am innocent of this man's blood", Matthew 27:24b. So Jesus was mocked, scourged, flogged and crucified.

The Resurrection

Just three days later, Jesus' tomb – a heavily guarded sealed rock crypt – was empty. It is upon the fact and the meaning of the empty tomb and the appearances afterward of the resurrected Christ that the Christian church has built its hope, its courage, its joy and its faith. For the risen Christ is, as the apostle Paul taught, the foundation stone of Christianity.

The Great Commission

Following His resurrection from the dead, in Jesus' final meeting with the apostles before He ascended into heaven, Jesus sent them out saying to them, "All authority in heaven and earth has been given to me. Therefore go and make disciples of all nations, baptising them in the name of the Father and of the Son and of the Holy Spirit, and teaching them to obey everything I have commanded you. And surely I am with you always, to the very end of the age", Matthew 28:18-20.

When Jesus ascended to his place with His Father, his followers now knew God's master plan for the human race, a plan of unending love. God was no longer a far away mystery; He had revealed his nature and character in Jesus, the God-man. As both God and man, Jesus reunited humanity to the timeless reality of God. As God, He was able to overcome sin and death. As a man, He enables mankind to share in His victory. Since Jesus, the Son of God, came down to us, died in our place and rose again, He enables us to share in His resurrection life, redeemed from sin, as children of God.

Jesus' Greatness

It was said of John the Baptist, "he will be great in the sight of the Lord", Luke 1:15; but of Jesus it was said, "He will be great", Luke 1:32. He is the great Prophet (Luke 7:16), the great God and Saviour (Titus 2:13), the great High Priest (Hebrews 4:14), and the great Shepherd of the sheep (Hebrews 13:20). According to Revelation 1:5, He is the faithful witness (the Prophet), the firstborn from the dead (the Priest) and the ruler over the kings of the earth (the King). He is also the Saviour of all those who trust in Him, who has made His people a kingdom of priests (Revelation 1:5b-6).

The Measure of His Love

We see the measure of Jesus' love in His selfless sacrifice on the cross. It is an extravagant love: His sweat became as drops of blood; the Roman soldiers struck Him in the face with their fists and with rods; they flogged Him with a Roman scourge; His beard was pulled out; thorns were pressed deep into His scalp; His hands and feet were pierced with nails; His side was pierced with a spear. In addition to this, however, the Bible tells us that upon Jesus at the cross was laid the sin of the whole world, God judged sin in Jesus, the sinless one, that He might extend mercy, grace and love to us, the sinful ones. That is the measure of Christ's love. It cost Him literally all He had. He offered Himself unblemished to God (Hebrews 9:14) when He laid down His life for us (John 10:11). It was His own life that He poured out in His blood as the redemptive price. Let us come to know that it is the measure of God's love.

He who went to the cross was the Son of God, and in this the greatest demonstration of God's love to man was expressed. "For God so loved the world that he gave his one and only Son, that whoever believes in him shall not perish but have eternal life" (John 3:16). This classic verse tells us of many great things: The great source of love – God; The great object of love – the world; The great gift of love – His only begotten Son; A great possibility of love – whosoever; A great condition of love – believes in Him; A great deliverance of love – shall not perish; A great possession of love – have everlasting life. Jesus Christ is Lord of all.

The Lordship of Jesus Christ

Christ is pre-eminent – first and foremost in everything – and the Christian's life should reflect that priority. As believers – who are rooted in Him, alive in Him, hidden in Him, complete in Him, clothed in His love, with His peace rules in our hearts – we are equipped to make Christ first in every area of life.

According to the book of Colossians, Jesus Christ is:

The Lord of creation (1:16-17)

The head over all rule and authority (2:10)

The author of reconciliation (1:20-22; 2:13-15)

The basis for the believer's hope, (1:5,23,27)

The source of the believer's power for a new life (1:11,29)

The believer's redeemer and reconciler (1:4, 20-22; 2:11-15)

The embodiment of full deity (1:15, 19; 2:9)

The Creator and sustainer of all things (1:16,17)

The head of the church (1:18)

The resurrected God-man (1:18; 3:1)

The all-sufficient Saviour (1:26; 2:3, 10; 3:1-4)

It is glorious to think, that now, through His death on the cross, we are made fit for the kingdom of God (1:12) and worthy to stand in the presence of God (1:22). Is Jesus not truly the "Wonderful Counsellor, Mighty God, everlasting Father, Prince of Peace?", Isaiah 9:6b.

Brief Explanation of His Lordship

It was by the Son that all things were created. This is true of all things in heaven and things in earth, of things seen and unseen. It was for the Son that all things were created. The Son is not only the agent of creation, He is also the goal of creation. That is to say, creation was created to be His. So, the Son is the beginning of creation, and the end of creation, and the power who holds creation together, the Creator, the sustainer and the final goal of the world.

Christ is the head of the church, which is His Body – So Jesus Christ is the guiding and governing influence of the church; it is at his bidding that the church must live and move. Christ is the source of the church's life and being. Jesus is someone who, because of his resurrection, is alive for evermore, and therefore the One whom we meet and experience. Christ is not a dead hero or a past founder, but a living person and presence. The result of all this is that he has the supremacy in all things. The resurrection of Jesus Christ is his title to supreme lordship. By his resurrection from the dead, he has shown that he has conquered every opposing power and that there is nothing in life or in death that can bind him. He is the living Lord; he is the source and origin of the church; he is the constant director of the church; and he is the Lord of all.

The object of His coming was reconciliation. He came to heal the rift and bridge the chasm between God and human beings. The act of reconciliation was the death of Jesus Christ. The medium of reconciliation was the blood of the cross. The power of reconciliation is the resurrection of Jesus Christ. The cross is the proof that there are no lengths to which the love of God will refuse to go in order to win human hearts. This is God's world and it is now a blood-bought, redeemed world, for – in some amazing way – God was in Christ reconciling the whole universe to Himself. We see from the above facts that the unchanging and unchangeable truth that Jesus Christ is Lord.

The total adequacy of the work of Christ – Sin is forgiven and evil is conquered. "…He forgave us all our sins, having cancelled the written code, with its regulations, that was against us and that stood opposed to us; he took it away, nailing it to the cross. And having disarmed the powers and authorities, he made a public spectacle of them, triumphing over them by the cross", Colossians 2:13b-15. God, in his amazing mercy, banished the record of our sins so completely that it was as if it had never been; not a trace remained. On the cross of Christ, the charge that was against us was itself crucified. Here indeed is grace.

Complete in Him

The One we have received when we are born again is 'Christ Jesus the Lord.' He is the Son of God who became Son of Man, and is "the blessed and only ruler, the King of kings and Lord of lords", 1 Timothy 6:15. "For this is what the high and lofty One says – he who lives forever, whose name is holy: 'I live in a high and holy place, but also with him who is contrite and lowly in spirit'", Isaiah 57:15. The double mystery of "you are in me, and I am in you", John 14:20, is the secret of the believer's joy, their confidence, their power, their "hope of glory", Colossians 1:27, and their completeness (2:10). The central consummating truth is contained in Colossians 2:10, we stand complete in him. Our head is in heaven, enthroned with God. Our citizenship is in heaven, to which we now belong, and our sole occupation should be with 'things above.'

Christ Is Our Life

With regard to the past, Christ "is our peace", Ephesians 2:14; in the present, He "is our life", Colossians 3:4; for the future, He "is our hope", 1 Timothy 1:1. It is a great title of devotion given to Christ in Colossians 3:4 Christ is our life. James posed a question, "What is your life?", James 4:14. Jesus said, in John 10:10b, "I have come that they may have life, and have it to the full." Paul's discovery and life experience was that "For to me, to live is Christ", Philippians 1:21, and that "it is no longer I who live but it is Christ who lives in me", Galatians 2:20. To Christians, Christ is the most important thing in life; more than this, He is life itself. Yes, Christ is their life. This is precisely why Christians set their minds and hearts on the things which are above and not on the things of this world

(Colossians 3:1-2). They judge everything in the light of the cross and in the light of the love that gave itself for them. Our life is hid with Christ in God.

Christ Is All and in All

In Summary, '1) In His Deity – He is the image of the invisible God; 2) In Creation – He is the Sovereign Creator of the universe; 3) In Pre-eminence – He is before all things; 4) In Redemption – He reconciled the universe through His blood; 5) In Headship – He has won a place over all principalities and powers; 6) In His church – He is the head of the body; 7) In His Indwelling Presence – He is the Christian hope. God has given Christ pre-eminence in all things. We dare not give Him a lower place!'[2]

Confess and Accept That Jesus Christ Is Lord

The title 'Lord', in Greek *kurios*, occurs in the New Testament well over 600 times. A day will come, when "at the name of Jesus every knee should bow, in heaven and on earth and under the earth, and every tongue confess that Jesus Christ is Lord, to the glory of God the Father", Philippians 2:10-11. The confession that Jesus Christ is Lord, and the belief in the resurrection, are necessary elements in salvation (Romans 10:9). It is only in and through the Holy Spirit that a man can say that Jesus Christ is Lord (1 Corinthians 12:3). The Christian in his heart must reverence Christ as Lord (1 Peter 3:15). Therefore, we accept Jesus as:

The absolute and undisputed owner and possessor of our lives, and that He is the Master, having absolute authority over all our lives, all our thoughts and all our actions.

The head of that great family in heaven and in earth of which God is the Father, and of which we, through Him have become a member.

The help of the helpless and the guardian of those who have no other to protect them.

He is the King and Emperor to whom we owe and give our constant homage, allegiance and loyalty.

He is the Divine One we must for ever worship and adore.

The early church summed up and affirmed its faith and belief in Jesus in the phrase 'Jesus Christ is Lord.' "In the beginning was the Word, and the Word was with God, and the Word was God", John 1:1. In Jesus Christ we see the very essence and being of God in human flesh – this is the reason why Jesus Christ is Lord. Our hearts cry out with Thomas with great discovery: "My Lord and my God!", John 20:28.

Concluding Remarks

Many within churches in the world today who are happy for Jesus to be a babe in a manger or, on the cross, the poor forsaken crucified Christ, a suffering Saviour, but not a risen, enthroned, reigning Lord and King Jesus Christ. We can easily settle for a watered down gospel of salvation. We want a Saviour, without a Lord and King. We want Him to be Saviour Jesus, not Lord and King Jesus; thus stripping away His Lordship, His rule, His authority over the lives of His people, of those who claim to love and know Him.

Jesus is the eternal Lord and King of the universe and without Him there is no forgiveness of sin, no life and no heaven, but only eternal separation from God and eternal judgement for sin. He is supreme in His nature for He is God who came in the flesh. He is infinite in His wisdom for He is the second person of the godhead. He is mighty in His majesty, He is perfect in His knowledge, He is complete in His power and He is pure in His character. He is majestic in His reign, righteous in His personality, merciful in His judgement and just in all His rulings. He is matchless in His sympathy, bountiful in His blessings, glorious in His splendour and impeccable in His reasoning, He is unique in His virgin birth, He is surpassing in His resurrection and He is from everlasting to everlasting.

What does this mean to us in our daily lives? It means that when we come to Jesus our Lord in worship, our eyes, our focus and our attention should be upon Him, our desire for Him, our love and affections toward Him, our hope in Him, our thankfulness and gratitude to Him, and our worship of Him.

Postscript: As I have finished writing this chapter, I had an encounter with the Lord Jesus. I heard a gentle whisper, 'Now you have completed this, am I really Lord of your life'? My eyes were filled with tears, deeply moved and touched by this question. I said, 'Lord, you know everything about me. Yes, you are my Lord forever.' Without Jesus there is no life. The question I want to ask my readers is this: 'Have you made Jesus Lord of your life'? If so, let us join in worship with the angels in heaven, "Holy, holy, holy is the Lord God Almighty, who was and is and is to come… You are worthy, our Lord and God, to receive glory and honour and power, for you created all things, and by your will they were created and have their being" (Revelation 4:8,11).

"Now that you know these things, you will be blessed if you do them", John 13:17.

Chapter 10

THE TRINITY

...love of God our Saviour appeared, he saved us....He saved us
through the washing of rebirth and renewal by the Holy Spirit, whom
he poured out on us graciously through Jesus Christ our Saviour.
(Titus 3:4-6)

Introduction

The doctrine of the Trinity is central to the Christian faith – it is key
to our understanding of the God we worship. In Exodus 3:13-14
(Moses and the burning bush), Moses expressed his concern about
the identity of God – God told him to tell the Israelites that 'I AM'
has sent you. An understanding of the name of God, who He is and
was, is important for faith. The doctrine held by most Christians is
that there are three Divine persons (Father, Son, and Holy Spirit)
united in the one Supreme Divine being. The essential truth which
leads to the doctrine of the Trinity can be shown in Scripture.

The Trinity is a way of acknowledging what the Bible reveals
to us about God, that God is three 'persons' who have the same

essence. God the Father is fully, completely God (1 Corinthians 8:6). God the Son (Jesus) is fully, completely God (John 1:1). And God the Holy Spirit is fully, completely God (1 Corinthians 6:19). Yet there is only one God. Jesus is not the Father (John 1:1), Jesus is not the Holy Spirit, The Father is not the Holy Spirit (Luke 3:21-22). In our world, with our limited human experience and imagination, it's challenging to understand the Trinity. But from the beginning we see God this way in the Scripture. Notice the plural pronouns 'us' and 'our' image in Genesis 1:26, "Let us make man in our image, in our likeness...".

Scriptural Basis for the Doctrine of Trinity

Old Testament teaching

"...Let us make man in our image, in our likeness ...", Genesis 1:26 (see also Genesis 3:22).

"...Whom shall I send? And who will go for us?", Isaiah 6:8.

"The Lord says to my lord, 'Sit at my right hand until I make your enemies a foot stool for your feet", Psalm 110:1. Jesus uses this passage to refer to Himself – the Christ (Matthew 22:41).

God's people rebelled and grieved his Holy Spirit. (Holy Spirit distinct from God Himself), Isaiah 63:10.

New Testament teaching

"Do not be afraid to take Mary home as your wife, because what is conceived in her is from the Holy Spirit", Matthew 1:20; Luke 1:35.

At Jesus' baptism, "At that moment heaven was opened, and he saw the Spirit of God descending like a dove and lighting on him. And a voice from heaven said, 'This is my Son, whom I love; with him I am well pleased", Matthew 3:16-17.

Great Commission, "...baptising them in the name of the Father and of the Son and of the Holy Spirit", Matthew 28:19-20.

"God has raised this Jesus to life, and we are all witnesses of the fact. Exalted to the right hand of God, he has received from the Father the promised Holy Spirit", Acts 2:32-33.

"Now there are varieties of gifts, by the same Spirit; and there are varieties of service, but the same Lord; and there are varieties of workings but it is the same God who inspires them all in everyone", 1 Corinthians 12:4-6 NASV.

"The grace of the Lord Jesus Christ, and the love of God, and the fellowship of the Holy Spirit be with you all", 2 Corinthians 13:14.

"Who have been chosen according to the foreknowledge of God the Father, through the sanctifying work of the Spirit, for obedience to Jesus Christ and sprinkling by his blood", 1 Peter 1:2.

Above Scriptures (and many more) support this doctrine of Trinity, since Scripture interprets Scripture.

God Is Three Persons

As I said earlier, the Father is not the Son; the Father is not the Holy Spirit; the Son is not the Holy Spirit. The Father, Son, and Holy Spirit are distinct persons.

In John chapter 1:1-2, we read "In the beginning was the Word, and the Word was with God, and the Word was God. He was with God in the beginning".

"The Word became flesh and made his dwelling among us... who came from the Father, full of grace and truth", John 1:14.

Jesus continues as our advocate, High Priest and intercessor at the right hand of God the Father (1 John 2:1 and Hebrews 7:25).

"But the Counsellor, the Holy Spirit, whom the Father will send in my name, will teach you all things and will remind you of everything I have said to you", John 14:26. The Father is not the Holy Spirit; the Son is not the Holy Spirit. We can see the Trinity is very clear in this text.

The Holy Spirit intercedes for us in accordance with the will of God (Romans 8:27).

"...Unless I go away, the Counsellor will not come to you; but if I go, I will send him to you", John 16:7.

God Is One

The Bible clearly speaks of: God the Father, God the Son, and God the Holy Spirit. But emphasises that there is only One God. The Scriptures that shows only One God, in Trinity:

"Hear, O Israel: The LORD is our God, the LORD is one.", Deuteronomy 6:4.

"I am the LORD, and there is no other; there is no God besides Me", Isaiah 45:5 NKJV.

"...there is no God but one", 1 Corinthians 8:4.

"For there is one God and there is one mediator between God and men, the Man Christ Jesus", 1 Timothy 2:5.

Each person is fully God

The Father

The Father is clearly God (Genesis 1:1, and throughout the Bible).

The Son

The Word was God, from the beginning (John 1:1-2, 14; Colossians 1:15).

Thomas referred to Jesus as 'My Lord and my God' (John 20:28).

"For in Christ all the fullness of the Deity lives in bodily form", Colossians 2:9.

"The Son is the radiance of God's glory and the exact representation of his being...", Hebrews 1:3.

"... the glorious appearing of our great God and Saviour, Jesus Christ", Titus 2:13.

"... the righteousness of our God and Saviour Jesus Christ", 2 Peter 1:1.

The Holy Spirit

The co-ordinating relationship of the Father, the Son, and the Holy Spirit demonstrates equality; therefore, if the Father and the Son are both God, then the Holy Spirit is also God (Matthew 28:19-20).

Lying to the Holy Spirit is lying to God (Acts 5:3-4).

"Where can I go from your Spirit? Where can I flee from your presence?" (Psalm 139:7).

Distinctions and Relationships between the Father, Son, and Holy Spirit

1. Different primary functions in relating to the world

Creation – The Father spoke the creative words; the Son (the Eternal Word) carried out the creative decrees (John 1:3; 1 Corinthians 8:6; Colossians 1:16; Hebrews 1:2); the Holy Spirit was active in sustaining and manifesting God's presence in creation (hovering over the waters – Genesis 1:2).

Redemption – The Father planned the redemption and sent His

Son into the world (John 3:16; Galatians 4:4; Ephesians 1:9-10). The Son obeyed the Father and accomplished redemption for us (John 6:38; Hebrews 10:5-7); after the Son's ascension, the Holy Spirit was sent by the Father and the Son to apply redemption to us (John 14:26). The Holy Spirit's role is to bring about regeneration – to bring to completion the work that has been planned by God the Father and begun by God the Son.

Father – planned and directed sending the Son and Holy Spirit.

Son and Holy Spirit are equal in Deity to God the Father, but they are subordinate in their roles for ever (1 Corinthians 15:28).

Salvation – Receiving Christ (John 1:12); Infilling of the Holy Spirit (John 7:37-38).

1 Peter 1:2 mentions all three members of the Trinity – God the Father, God the Son (Jesus Christ) and God the Holy Spirit. All members of the Trinity work to bring about our Salvation. The Father chose us before we chose him (Ephesians 1:4). Jesus Christ the Son died for us while we were still sinners (Romans 5:6-1). The Holy Spirit brings us the benefits of Salvation and sets us apart (sanctifies us) for God's service (2 Thessalonians 2:13).

2. God eternally existed as Father, Son, and Holy Spirit

Before all eternity – (Father had been and is, and will be Father); The Son has always been the Son, the Holy Spirit has always been the Holy Spirit.

No difference in Deity – attributes or essential nature between the Father, Son and Holy Spirit. "The only distinction between the members of the Trinity are in the ways they relate to each other and to the rest of creation – eternal equality in being but subordination in role"[1].

Importance of the Trinity – At the Heart of the Christian Faith.

Atonement – If Jesus is merely a created being then he could not bear the full wrath of God.

Justification by faith alone – If Jesus is not God then we cannot rely on him alone to save us.

Praying and worshipping Jesus – If he is not God, then we cannot do this; yet the New Testament commands us to do so. (Philippians 2:9-11; Revelation 5:12-14).

If Jesus saves us but is not God, then salvation would be credited to a created being, (exalting the created rather than the Creator).

Concluding Remarks

What does it mean to us?

God is Awesome! He is beyond our complete understanding. But the personal relationship within the Trinity shows that we can (and should) have a personal relationship with God. He is the God of the universe! His ways are above our ways (Isaiah 55:8). We need to focus on, and seek His righteousness (Matthew 6:33).

Unity of the Church (The Body of Christ) – We are made to be part of God's church. The body is a unit, though it is made up of many parts; though all its parts are many, they form one body (1 Corinthians 12:12):

Unity in the Body of Christ – diverse gifts, nations, tribes, races.

Our unity glorifies God by reflecting something of the unity and diversity of the Trinity (Psalm 133).

Jesus' prayer for unity – "I in them and you in me. May they be brought to complete unity to let the world know that you sent me and have loved them even as you have loved me", John 17:23.

This unity is a means to reach out to the world.

Prayer and worship – is to be directed to God the Father through God the Son, by the guidance and empowerment of the Holy Spirit.

In Christ's Second Coming we will see the culmination of God's redemption – which has been planned, executed and sustained by the Triune God.

To sum up the Trinity, it is a description of the unique relationship of God the Father, the Son, and the Holy Spirit. In the Gospels, at Jesus' baptism, the Spirit descended like a dove on Jesus, and the voice from heaven proclaimed the Father's approval of Jesus as His divine Son. That Jesus is God's divine Son and is the foundation for all we read about Jesus in the Gospels. Here we see all three members of the Trinity together. God eternally exists as three persons – Father, Son, and Holy Spirit; each person is fully God and there is one God. Our Triune God's attributes are: love, holiness, constancy, justice, truth, eternality, omniscience (all-knowing), omnipresence (all-present), and omnipotence (all-powerful). We are created in the image of God – interdependent. We are created to love God – God is love and loving.

The Bible reveals God's personality, His character and His plan for His creation. It also reveals God's deepest desire to relate to and fellowship with the people He created. We can know this God who created the universe in a very personal way through His Son, Jesus Christ and through His Word. Psalm 19 is a magnificent portrayal of God. 'In this Psalm, three ways in which God reveals Himself: 1) In creation (vv 1-6) – The beauty and precision of creation displays the Creator's eternal power and godhead. 2) In the Scriptures (vv 7-11) – The psalmist uses six titles and seven attributes, and six results from obeying it. 3) To the seeking soul (vv 12-14) – In our heart as we worship Him'[2]. "May the words of mouth and the meditation of my heart be pleasing in your sight, O LORD, my Rock and my Redeemer", v 14.

Chapter 11

THE LOVE OF GOD

How great is the love the Father has lavished on us,
that we should be called children of God! (1 John 3:1)

Introduction

God loves us so much that He sent Jesus to die in our place giving us the life of His Son freely. He did this knowing full well the awful cost to Himself. God's love is always manifested through action. He loves us more than we can comprehend and has given us through the incredible benefits of the Blood Covenant. Even in the old covenant He admonished us not to forget His benefits. We read in Psalm 103, "Praise the LORD, O my soul, and forget not all his benefits – who forgives all your sins and heals all your diseases, who redeems your life from the pit and crowns you with love and compassion, who satisfies your desires with good things so that your youth is renewed like the eagles"(vv 2-5). In Jeremiah 31:3 NLT, God said to His people, "I have loved you, my people, with an everlasting love. With unfailing love I have drawn you to myself". God reaches toward us with kindness motivated by deep and everlasting love.

Tony Campolo, a worldwide traveller and speaker says, 'God loves you when you have done well. He's pleased when you have accomplished something worthwhile. But the news is that He loves you even when you haven't done well. He loves you even when you mess things up. He loves you when you have done terrible things. He loves you even when you have done the most despicable things imaginable. In spite of anything you might have done God still loves you. In spite of what you are, God still loves you. That's what God's love (agape) is all about'[1]. May I challenge you to believe it and experience it with a thankful heart. 'God loves each one of us as if there was only one of us to love' (St. Augustine). Let us learn together that spiritual blessings are the principal gifts of Divine love. How blessed to know that when the world hates us, God loves us!

The Nature of God

There are three things told us in Scripture concerning the nature of God. 1) God is 'spirit' (John 4:24). God has no visible substance. Had God a tangible body, He would not be omnipresent; He would be limited to one place; because He is spirit He fills heaven and earth. 2) God is light (1 John 1:5), which is opposite of 'darkness'. In Scripture darkness stands for sin, evil, death; and 'light' for holiness, goodness and life. God is light, means that He is the sum of all excellence. 3) God is 'love' (1 John 4:8). It not simply that God 'loves', but that He is love itself. There are many today who talk about the love of God, who are total strangers to the God of love. Our hearts need to be so occupied with His wondrous love for His people. The better we are acquainted with

His love – its nature, fullness, blessedness – the more will our hearts be drawn out in love to Him. Stated below are some broad aspects of God's love:

God's love is uninfluenced. The love of God is free, spontaneous, uncaused. "The LORD did not set his love on you nor chose you because you were more in number .... but because the LORD loves you ...", Deuteronomy 7:7-8 NKJV. He loves from Himself – according to His own purpose and grace (2 Timothy 1:9 NKJV). "We love Him, because He first loved us", 1 John 4:19 NKJV. Because He loved us when we were loveless, it is clear that His love was uninfluenced.

God's love is sovereign. This is self-evident as God Himself is sovereign and under obligation to none, a law unto Himself, acting always according to His own imperial pleasure. Since God is sovereign, and since He is love, it necessarily follows that His love is sovereign. The sovereignty of God's love necessarily follows from the fact that it is uninfluenced (Ephesians 1:4-5).

God's love is eternal. God Himself is eternal, and God is love; therefore, as God Himself had no beginning, nor end. How clear is the testimony of Jeremiah 31:3 NKJV, "Yes, I have loved you with an everlasting love; Therefore with loving kindness I have drawn you"; " I have loved you deeply," says the LORD, Malachi 1:2 NLT. Since God's love toward us had no beginning it can have no ending! Since it be true that from 'everlasting to everlasting' He is God, and since God is love, then it is equally true that from everlasting to everlasting He loves His people.

God's love is infinite. Everything about God is infinite. His essence fills heaven and earth. His wisdom is unlimited, for He knows everything of the past, present and future. His power is unbounded, for there is nothing too hard for Him. So His love is without limit. (Ephesians 2:4). No tongue can fully express the infinitude of God's love, or any mind comprehend it, it passes knowledge (Ephesians 3:19).

God's love is immutable. As with God Himself there is "no variableness, neither shadow of turning", James 1:17, so His love knows neither change nor diminution. "For I am the LORD, I do not change", Malachi 3:6 NKJV.

God's love is holy. God's love is not regulated by passion, or sentiment, but by principle. God's love never conflicts with His holiness. His love is pure, unmixed with any sentimentality.

God's love is gracious. The love and favour of God are inseparable. This is clearly brought out in Romans 8:32-39. Christ died not in order to make God love us, but because He did love His people, Calvary is the supreme demonstration of His Divine love.

Demonstration of God's Love

Jesus, who went to the cross was the Son of God, and in this the greatest demonstration of God's love to man was expressed in John 3:16 (NLT), "For God so loved the world that he gave his only Son, so that everyone who believes in him will not perish but have eternal life". This verse has been called everybody's text as well as the greatest statement in the Bible. In this most used popular text reveals the extravagant love of God:

'God' – the greatest lover/person and a great source of love

'so loved the world' – the greatest degree of devotion and the greatest number. This tells us that God's kingdom is not limited to any single nation or race.

'that he gave' – the greatest act

'his only Son' – the greatest gift

'everyone' – the greatest invitation and greatest possibility

'who believes' – the greatest simplicity with a greatest condition

'in him' – the greatest person

'will not perish' – the greatest mercy and deliverance

'but' – the greatest difference

'have' – the greatest certainty

'eternal life' – the greatest possession/result

The initiative in all salvation of man lies with God. It was with God that it all started. It was God who sent His son, and he sent him, because he loved the world he had created. At the centre of everything is the love of God. The mainspring of God's being is love. Isn't it wonderful that God acting not for his own sake but for ours in order to satisfy his love. God is our Father who cannot be happy until his wandering children have come home. We can clearly see in this passage the width of the love of God. It was the world that God so loved. Indeed, it was the world: the unlovable and the unlovely, the lonely who have no one else to love them. It excites me to think and feel that all are included in this vast inclusive love of God. This amazing love of God is unquestionable, its power unconquerable, its meaning undeniable, its price unimaginable, its absence unthinkable.

How can we comprehend what is 'an everlasting love': God's love for us has no beginning and no ending; God will never stop loving us; there is nothing we can do to make God love us more, and there is nothing that we can do to make God love us less; God loves us with an everlasting love; God draws us to Himself with unfailing love.

Matthew Henry says, 'Jesus Christ came to save us by pardoning us, that we might not die by the sentence of the law. Here is gospel, good news indeed. Here is God's love in giving his Son for the world. God so loved the world; so really, so richly. The great gospel duty is to believe in Jesus Christ. Here is the great gospel benefit, that whoever believes in Christ, shall not perish, but shall have everlasting life. God sent one to save us, who was dearest to himself; and shall he not be dearest to us?'[2]

God's Immeasurable and Inexhaustible Love

How powerfully the apostle Paul speaks of the love of Christ in Ephesians 3:18-19. God's love is total, says Paul. It reaches every corner of our experience. '....to grasp how wide and long and high and deep is the love of Christ, and to know this love that surpasses knowledge...':

God's love is wide – It covers the breadth of our own experience, and it reaches out to the whole world and ranks.

God's love is long – It continues the length of our lives and from everlasting to everlasting.

God's love is high – It rises to the heights of our celebration, elation to happiness and glory.

God's love is deep – It reaches to the depth of discouragement, despair, and even who are sunk into the depths of sin and misery and death.

We can never be lost to God's love. Believers have always had to face hardships in many forms. But as apostle Paul exclaims that it is impossible to be separated from Christ. His death for us is proof of

His unconquerable love. "....we are more than conquerors through him who loved us...., neither height nor depth, nor anything else in all creation, will be able to separate us from the love of God that is in Christ Jesus our Lord", Romans 8:37-39. Paul speaks as one amazed, and swallowed up in admiration, wondering at the height and depth, and length and breadth, of the love of Christ which passes knowledge. God having manifested His love in giving His own Son for us, can we think that anything should turn aside or do away with that love.

Redeeming Love

We must not neglect the central theme of the gospel: God's redeeming, all-embracing, utterly limitless love. Apostle John writes in 1 John 4:7-11, "...let us love one another, for love comes from God. Everyone who loves has been born of God and knows God. Whoever does not love does not know God, because God is love. This is how God showed his love among us: He sent his one and only Son into the world that we might live through him. This is love: not that we loved God, but that he loved us and sent his Son as an atoning sacrifice for our sins". John adds, "God is love". "... We love because he first loved us" (vv 16-19). How did Jesus love us? He gave Himself for us.

What motivated God to send Jesus?

John says, 'God is love'. Love is a choice and an action. God is the source of our love (1 Corinthians 13:4-7): He loved us enough to sacrifice His Son for us. "But God demonstrates his own love for us in this: While we were still sinners, Christ died for us", Romans 5:8:

God created us because He loves us, He created us to love Him.

God cares about us because He loves us and He cares for sinful people.

We are free to choose to love Him because God wants a loving response from us.

Christ died because of His love for us caused Him to seek a solution to the problem of sin. Jesus the Son of God came in the form of a human being and took the punishment for sin and its consequences on Himself. He took our place.

We receive eternal life because God's love expresses itself to us forever.

Revelation of God's Love

David had a revelation of God's great love for him. He was absolutely grounded in it. He wasn't afraid to turn to Him regardless of what was going on. He messed up many times yet in the midst of the messes, David would time after time turn back to Him and rest in his great love. The apostle John referred to himself several times in the book of John as 'the disciple whom Jesus loved'. What a revelation of the love of God he had.

Our Response to God's Love

How can we possibly love God as much as He loves us? The Bible says that the love of God is shed abroad in our hearts by the Holy Spirit (Romans 5:5):

Love – The Bible says, "'You shall love the Lord your God with all your heart, and with all your soul, and with all your strength, and with all your mind, and your neighbour as yourself'", Luke 10:27; Deuteronomy 6:5 NKJV. So where does that love begin? Loving God begins with sincerely being grateful for all He has done for us: creating us, sending Christ to die for us, choosing us, to live with Him in heaven and giving us the Holy Spirit. Loving God begins in our heart and is eventually shown through our actions by coming ourselves completely to Him.

Obedience – We can express our love to God like Jesus did, through obedience to His written Word and what He tells us to do: "If you love me, you will obey what I command"; "Whoever has my commands and obeys them, he is the one who loves me"; "If anyone loves me, he will obey my teaching. My Father will love him, and we will come to him and make our home with him", John 14:15, 21, 23. Loving God means being willing to do whatever He asks and by loving Him more than any relationship, activity, achievement, or possession. Love is more than lovely words; It is commitment and conduct. If we love Christ then prove it by obeying what He says in His Word.

Thankfulness – We can express our gratitude to God by thanking him for everything he has done for us and for his great love. "Therefore by Him let us continually offer the sacrifice of praise to God, that is, the fruit of our lips, giving thanks to His name", Hebrews 13:15 NKJV. (see also Colossians 1:12, 3:17). A 'sacrifice of praise' would include thanking Christ for his sacrifice on the cross and would lead to telling others about it.

Believing Him – The Bible clearly tells us what pleases our Father God and believing what He says is one of them. This is called faith. "And without faith it is impossible to please God, because anyone who comes to him must believe that he exists and that he rewards those who earnestly seek him", Hebrews 11:6.

Love one another – Our job is to love faithfully the people God has given to us to love. The real test of our love for God is how we treat the people right in front of us – our family members and fellow believers. We cannot truly love God while neglecting to love those who are created in His image. God is the source of all human love, and spreads like fire. Christ commands us to love others as He loved us. "My command is this: Love each other as I have loved you", John 15:12. This love is evidence that we are truly saved. God is love; He cares that His children love each other.

Concluding Remarks

Everyone talks about love. We want to be loved, to 'fall in' love and find somebody to love. But if we want to know real love, we should check out God's love for us. His love for us is unconditional, unselfish, giving, and sacrificial. God is the source of real love. When we trust in Christ, God gives us the ability to love others His way. When God loves, He loves the world; when God gives, He gives His Son; and when God saves, He saves for ever as we saw earlier in John 3:16. God is love. His ways are the ways of peace and life and love for all mankind. His love is infinite and eternal; yet His love is focused on each individual.

Christ's command is for Christians to love one another. This is the basic ingredient of true Christianity. The love of God is well expressed in the song written by Frederick M Lehman (1948):

"The love of God is greater far,

Than tongue or pen can ever tell;

It goes beyond the highest star,

And reaches the lowest hell,

The guilty pair, bowed down with care,

God gave His Son to win;

His erring child He reconciled,

And pardoned from his sin.

Refrain O Love of God, how rich and pure!

How measureless and strong!

It shall for evermore endure

The saints' and angels' song.

When years of time shall pass away,

And earthly thrones and kingdoms fall,

When men, who here refuse to pray,

On rocks and hills and mountains call,

God's love so sure, shall still endure,

All measureless and strong;

Redeeming grace to Adam's race –

The saints' and angels' song"[3].

Chapter 12

HAVE FAITH IN GOD

"Have faith in God", Jesus answered. (Mark 11:22)

Introduction

A sinner cannot be saved apart from faith (Hebrews 4:2; Ephesians 2:8-9). "For it is by grace you have been saved, through faith. . .and it is the gift of God", Ephesians 2:8. It is vitally important that we should find out what 'having faith in God' means. In the Bible, faith is personal confidence in God. It means that we believe what He says, and trust Him to save us and keep us. Faith is a gift of God (Ephesians 2:8; Hebrews 12:2). God gives men the power to believe in Him. God has promised that any man who wishes to do His will, come to a knowledge of the truth (John 7:17). Faith must be placed in a trust worthy object.

Christianity is based on relationship with a living person of God. Therefore, we need to know something about Him in order to have an accurate concept of God. The valid and the only source for this is through the Word of God. Therefore, it is important for us to find out for ourselves through the Word, God's character and basis for trustworthiness.

Reasons We Can Have Faith in God

One reason we can have faith in God because He is faithful. We can trust God because He is trustworthy:

God's position – God is seated on his throne in His majesty as the Creator of the Universe. "The LORD has established his throne in heaven, and his kingdom rules over all" (Psalm 103:19; see also Revelation 4:1).

God's power – God has absolute power (Luke 1:37; Luke 18:27). "Ah, Sovereign LORD, you have made the heavens and the earth by your great power and outstretched arms. Nothing is too hard for you", Jeremiah 32:17.

God's resources – "The earth is the Lord's and everything in it, the world, and all who live in it", Psalm 24:1. "Sovereign Lord", they said, "you made the heaven and the earth and the sea, and everything in them", Acts 4:24, (see also Psalm 50:10; Haggai 2:8).

God's Character and Nature – God is good and He does good. "Every good and perfect gift is from above, coming down from the Father of the heavenly lights. . .", James 1:17. "I will make an everlasting covenant with them: I will never stop doing good to them. . .I will rejoice in doing them good.....with all my heart and soul", Jeremiah 32:40-41, (see also Psalm 34:8; 86:5). We must be fully persuaded that God is good.

God is rich in mercy – (Psalm 103:8-13). "As a father has compassion on his children, so the LORD has compassion on those who fear him", Psalm 103:13. He forgives us when we ask Him. He is merciful and ready to forgive. "If we confess our sins, he is faithful and just and will forgive us our sins and purify us from all unrighteousness", 1 John 1:9.

God is faithful – He is dependable, can count on him. Because God is faithful, it enables us to trust him. "God is faithful, by whom you were called into the fellowship of His Son, Jesus Christ our Lord", 1 Corinthians 1:9 NKJV. "...Great is Your faithfulness", Lamentations 3:23, (see also 2 Thessalonians 3:3).

God is unchanging – He is constant. "I the LORD do not change", Malachi 3:6. James 1:17 tells us "...the Father of the heavenly lights who does not change like shifting shadows".

God is willing – Is God willing to use all that He is and all that He has for us? Matthew 6:25-34 shows that the heavenly Father will provide for us and He is willing to meet our needs. "But seek first his kingdom and his righteousness, and all these things will be given to you as well", v 33. Yes, He is willing. In Mark 1:41 NKJV, Jesus replied "I am willing; be cleansed" to the leper who wanted to know if Jesus would heal him. The Bible reveals Jesus to be the visible manifestation of God; thereby allowing us to see what God is like towards us. "The Son is the radiance of God's glory and the exact representation of his being, sustaining all things by his powerful word...", Hebrews 1:3a.

Faith Explained

As we have already considered, to have faith is to be fully convinced of the truthfulness and reliability of that in which we believe. Faith in God is having the kind of trust and confidence in God and in Christ that leads us to commit our whole being to Him as Saviour and Lord. The Bible says, "Now faith is the substance of things hoped for, the evidence of things not seen", Hebrews 11:1 NKJV. When we have this spiritual substance in us, it communicates to us a certain inner knowing that the thing we are hoping for is certainly established, even before we see any natural evidence that it has happened.

Faith in God is a response to God's word which moves God to act. Jesus said in Mark 11:23-24 NKJV, "For assuredly, I say to you, whoever says to this mountain, 'Be removed and be cast into the sea', and does not doubt in his heart, but believes that those things he says will be done, he will have whatever he says. Therefore I say to you, whatever things you ask when you pray, believe that you receive them, and you will have them". Words mixed with the real, pure faith, can and will move mountains or any other problem that we face.

Faith in God must be from the heart. It is spiritual. "For it is with your heart that you believe and are justified, and it is with your mouth that you confess and are saved", Romans 10:10. Hope is a condition for faith. Hope is positive unwavering expectation of good. It keeps us in the place where we can believe, but it is not in itself 'faith'. Yet, without hope there are no 'things hoped for'.

The Reasons Why We need Faith
Why Must We Believe God?

The Bible says:

"And without faith it is impossible to please God, because anyone who comes to him must believe that he exists and he rewards those who earnestly seek him", Hebrews 11:6.

"...everything that does not come from faith is sin", Romans 14:23b and God hates sin. When we don't believe God, we treat him like he is a liar. Let us remember that He is everywhere and sees all things. God is hurt when we act like He doesn't exist, or that He will not do what He promised to do. Only when we have confidence in God and in His Word can we please Him.

God's commands can only really be fulfilled through faith. Lack of faith leads to a lack of obedience. Lack of obedience in God's eyes is rebellion. Disobedience dishonours God. Without confidence in God's promises, we will never really do what God says.

We are designed by God to live by faith. "We live by faith, not by sight", 2 Corinthians 5:7. "The righteous will live by faith", Romans 1:17b. Therefore live a life of righteousness, we must live by faith.

It is one of the foundational doctrines of the Christian faith. "...not laying again the foundation of repentance. . .and of faith in God", Hebrews 6:1.

It is one of the basic ingredients for a fruitful Christian life. "For this very reason make every effort to add to your faith goodness. . . and you will receive a rich welcome into the eternal kingdom of our Lord and Saviour Jesus Christ", 2 Peter 1:5-12.

Benefits of Faith

The Bible teaches us that genuine faith is "more precious than gold that perishes", 1 Peter 1:7 NKJV :

Faith brings salvation – (Ephesians 2:8-9). "....who ever believes in him shall not perish but have eternal life", John 3:16. (see also John 5:24; Romans 1:17).

Faith brings answers to prayer – "If you believe, you will receive whatever you ask for in prayer", Matthew 21:22). Jesus taught us to pray for our daily bread (Matthew 6:11), faith is therefore key to our daily provision.

Faith brings all the benefits of salvation into our lives – (Ephesians 2:8-9). This includes healing, prosperity, peace, love, and joy (1 Peter 1:8).

Faith is a major key to effective ministry for Christ (Matthew 17:19-21). He (Jesus) replied, "Because you have so little faith. I tell you the truth if you have faith as small as a mustard seed, you can say to this mountain, 'Move from here to there' and it will move. Nothing will be impossible for you," Matthew 17:20-21.

Accessing Faith

How do we access the provision that God has for us? The key is, believing according to what the Scripture tells us. Believing God or having faith is the most 'natural attitude' for a believer to have. Faith is a fruit of the Spirit (Galatians 5:22), and so we have a measure of it when we are born-again. 2 Peter 2:5 says "....make every effort to add to your faith...". Now let us look at knowing what God has said as a basis for believing. As mentioned earlier, Hebrews 11:1 tells us that 'faith is evidence'. The Word of God is the evidence that we base our believing on and our job is to collect evidence. When we abide in God and His word in us, we can ask what we desire and it shall be done for us according to John 15:7. We must 'soak' ourselves in and meditate upon the Scriptures that we are basing our believing on until we have faith in our heart about the subject. To develop such faith, we must listen to the Word of God as much as possible. "Faith comes by hearing, and hearing by the word of God", Romans 10:17 NKJV. The book of Proverbs encourages us to constantly keep the word in our hearts and keep our attention on it (4:20-22). We should make sure that our heart in a place of confidence before we release our faith.

How Do We Release Our Faith

The way we release our faith takes us back to Mark 11:23-24. One way of releasing our faith is by speaking (v 23). The reason why this works is that spiritual truth is higher than that of natural reality. Everything in the natural was created by the spiritual through the spoken word (Hebrews 11:3; Genesis 1:3-6). This means that through believing and speaking the Word which is spiritual truth, we can align our natural circumstances, to the Will of God for our lives based on His word and our new relationship with him as sons. 'God calls the things that are not as though they were' (Romans 4:17) and we can do the same. When we have faith in our heart we can release it through the words of our mouth and it will produce result. Jesus put this principle into operation when He cursed the fig tree and it withered through the power of His words spoken in faith (Matthew 21: 18-22). Jesus also spoke to the storm and it was stilled; the sick and they were healed; the dead and they were raised. Jesus said that we could speak to mountains and they would be removed.

Another way of releasing our faith is found in verse 24 and that is asking and believing that we receive when we ask and having that which we ask for. Often there can be a transition time between the moment of asking and the manifestation of the thing in the natural. What we do in that situation is to start thanking God for the thing we have received (Philippians 2:6-7). We also have to 'hold fast to the profession of our faith without wavering' according to Hebrews 10:23. When we profess the truth with our mouths, it is a means to harness our minds.

We must make sure that we walk in forgiveness and in love. "And when we stand praying, if you hold anything against anyone, forgive him, so that your Father in heaven may forgive you your sins", Mark 11:25-26. "...The only thing that counts is faith expressing itself through love", Galatians 5:6b. When we have asked God, we need to enter into the rest of knowing that we have it. Part of this is to rejoice with a thankful heart towards God (Philippians 4:4-7; Psalm 32:11).

Hindrances to Faith

Ignorance – (1 Timothy 1:13) Much unbelief rises out of lack of knowledge and understanding of the Word of God. It can be that the Scriptures have been wrongly taught or not known at all.

Not accepting God's Word as the final authority – This can be motivated by pride and a rebellious attitude. The cure for this therefore is to humble oneself and change one's mind, choosing to believe what the Scripture says.

Fear – Negative fear gives rise to negative emotions. It is rooted in anxiety and lack of trust in God's Fatherly protection and love. Perfect love cast out all fear (1 John 4:18). God is perfect love.

Doubt – (Matthew 14:31) Doubt is a real hindrance to faith because it speaks with a voice that challenges the truth or the reality of what we should be believing. To overcome this we must fill ourselves with the Word of God, meditating deeply on it and deciding to believe the Word over the things that we see, hear and feel.

Discouragement – Sometimes we are discouraged because of physical or emotional weakness or past experiences. To overcome this we must make a decision to be strong in the Lord (Hebrews 12:12; Ephesians 6:10).

The love of praise from others – (John 12:43) To overcome this, we must cultivate a personal relationship with God through prayer and obedience. We must allow our old nature to be weakened as we say 'yes' to God and 'no' to the desire for getting praise and recognition.

Working Our Faith

Let us put our faith to work. When we put our faith into action, God will work on our behalf. When it feels like we are down for the count of ten, we have to rise up and say, "I shall not die but live, and declare the works of the Lord", Psalm 118:17 NKJV. That kind of faith gets God's attention every time. When my son-in-law was seriously ill and confined to bed for a number of days, he declared over his life in faith very frequently, 'I will not die but live'. Subsequently, he made a rapid and complete recovery from his illness.

Naaman the leper a popular commander in the Syrian army, humbled himself and became willing to listen to a servant girl and a seemingly strange instruction from a prophet of God. "So he went down and dipped himself in the Jordan seven times, as the man of God had told him, and his flesh was restored and became clean like that of a young boy", 2 Kings 5:14. Faith says, I don't care where I have to go, what I have to do or who I have to listen to, whatever God says, I will do (2 Kings 5:1-19).

Our 'faith' is what activates the power of God. The Bible says, 'these trials will show that your faith is genuine' (1 Peter 1:7). "Through your faith God is protecting you by his power", 1 Peter 1:5 NLT. Personally, I am recipient of this grace as I faced having to give up my much loved professional life due to a surgical procedure that went wrong and left me disabled in the month of March 1991. We need to 'take up the shield of faith' and stop all the flaming arrows of the evil one'. Also, take "...the sword of the Spirit, which is the word of God", Ephesians 6:16-17. Sometimes, when we are losing our life, our family, our joy, our finances and our health, it is time to cry out, 'Jesus, have mercy on me!'. Away with dignity and decorum, desperate people pray desperate prayers and God responds to their prayers. We have to do what David did; "I cried to the LORD with my voice, and He heard me from His holy hill", Psalm 3:4 NKJV. So, let's put our faith to work.

The faith that God responds to does not require explanations. The ten lepers Jesus healed (Luke 17:11-14), "And as they went they were cleansed" when Jesus said "Go and show yourselves to the priests". Indeed, when Jesus tells us to do something it may not seem like it is even related to what we are praying about at all. When that happens, we have a decision to make: doubt Him or obey Him. The Bible says, "The steps of a good man are ordered by the LORD", Psalm 37:23 NKJV. When God tells us something let us step out on it. Walk the walk of faith. Rise up in faith and declare, 'I am forgiven, I am healed, I am redeemed, I am satisfied, I am crowned with love and compassion and I am renewed' (Psalm 103:2-5).

Concluding Remarks

Faith means to believe; to fully trust in; to have confidence; to have assurance; to have reliance; to have conviction. Faith means both to believe and be faithful to that belief, to be faithful and trust worthy; to be loyal and steadfast in devotion and allegiance, constant, enduring. We cannot trust God without knowing him. Faith has to be in two places – in our heart and in our mouth. First we must agree in our head with what the Bible says in order to get it into our heart. Then it has to be in our heart to such a degree that it overflows and this only happens by spending time seeking God and His Word. Faith that moves mountains is simply trusting God to keep His word. Jesus said in John 14:12-14, "Most assuredly, I say to you, he who believes in Me the works that I do he will do also; and greater works than these he will do, because I go to My Father. And whatever you ask in

My name, that I will do, that the Father may be glorified in the Son. If you ask anything in My name, I will do it", (NKJV).

When we study Matthew chapter nine we can see faith in action in the following examples. The daughter was raised from the dead because of the father's faith (9:18-26). The women with issue of blood, was healed and saved because of her own faith (9:20-22). Two blind men received their sight because of their persistent faith (9:27-31). The dumb man possessed by an evil spirit was delivered and received his sanity because of the faith of others (9:32-33).

Finally, faith is founded on divine truth (God's promise) and is witnessed to by the spirit in the heart because we have within us the Holy Spirit and He is the source of our faith.

Chapter 13

THE WORD OF GOD – THE BIBLE

Your word is a lamp to my feet and a light for my path.
(Psalm 119:105)

Introduction

This is a bewildering age. People lack a sense of direction and destiny. The message of God's Word is the total answer to man's total need. It is the good news of love, forgiveness, faith, peace, purpose and heaven. In the Bible, man discovers what he is to believe and where he is going. It is in the Holy Scriptures that we find the answers to life's ultimate questions: Where did I come from, why am I here, where am I going and what is the purpose of my existence?

The message of the Bible is the message of Jesus Christ who said, "I am the way, the truth, and the life", John 14:6. It is a story of salvation, the story of redemption through Christ, the story of life, of peace and of eternity. The Bible is so old yet it is ever new. It contains sixty six books written over a period of several hundred years by many different men, divinely inspired by the Holy Spirit. It consists of the Old Testament - 39 books and the New Testament - 27 books. The Bible, the greatest document available for the human race, needs to be opened, read and believed. It was written only that we might believe and understand, know and love, and follow and obey Christ the Living Word. The Bible is a gift to us because:

It is personal that is, 'All Scripture is God-breathed' (inspired);

It is practical (useful) – 'is useful for teaching, rebuking, correcting and training in righteousness';

It is provisional – 'so that the man of God may be thoroughly equipped for every good work' (2 Timothy 3:16-17).

What the Bible Has to Say about Itself

God is its author – It is God's word, not man's! It is originated by Him. "....when you received the word of God, which you heard from us, you accepted it not as the word of men, but as it actually is, the word of God which is at work in you who believe", 1 Thessalonians 2:13. Think of it and receive it as God's word with hunger and thirst. Double-minded people are unstable people (James 1:8), and unstable people eventually fall. If we put God's Word first in our lives, we will hold up and we will not fall (James 1:16-17; 2 Peter 3:17-18; Jude 20-25). Let us cultivate a holy fear of the Lord and His Word (Psalm 119:20) and we will not be ashamed of our hope (Psalm 119:16).

The Word of God is creative – "...by God's word the heavens existed and the earth was formed", 2 Peter 3:5. His word alone was enough to create all that exists. He doesn't have to strive or sweat, He just has to say it and it is done. We must also speak God's word!

The Word of God is authoritative – "They were astonished at His teaching, for His word was with authority. . .they were all amazed saying",... "what a word this is! For with authority and power He commands the unclean spirits, and they came out", Luke 4:36 NKJV. The forces of darkness around us must recognise and submit to God's authoritative Word. So let us stand on it firmly.

The Word of God is effective – "...my word....will not return to me empty, but will accomplish what I desire and achieve the purpose for which I sent it", Isaiah 55:11. Every word God speaks is on a mission and is guaranteed to accomplish it in accordance with His will, His strategy and His timing. So let us put God's word to work in our lives.

The Word of God is dynamic – "...The words I have spoken to you are spirit and they are life", John 6:63. When we receive it as the word of God, it produces life-changing results. It can't just sit there and do nothing, it must generate, for "....when you received the word of God, which you heard from us, you accepted it not as the word of men, but as it actually is, the word of God, which is at work in you who believe", 1 Thessalonians 2:13'.[1]

The Word of God is permanent – For us to get the maximum benefit of God's Word, we must receive it as permanent and eternal word of God not a temporary word. "Heaven and earth will pass away, but my words will never pass away", Mark 13:31. It never needs updating; it is perfect and can't be improved upon. That is why Jesus instructs us to let "my words remain in you" John 15:7.

The Word of God is alive, powerful and active – "For the word of God is living and active. Sharper than any double-edged sword, it penetrates even to dividing soul and spirit, joints and marrow; it judges the thoughts and attitudes of the heart", Hebrews 4:12. Yes, God's Word is living and active. It is the voice of God speaking to us. It is able to penetrate our lives and reveal our hearts and the attitudes in our hearts. A major way it does this is by our response to His word and His voice.

We have to 'programme our mind with the scriptures' to benefit the blessings from the Word of God: "Let the word of Christ dwell in you richly....", Colossians 3:16. That is to say, be filled with the Word of God; and "Do not let this book of the Law depart from your mouth; meditate on it day and night....do everything written in it. Then you will be prosperous and successful", Joshua 1:8. To retain it permanently, read it regularly, gratefully, dependently and carefully. The message of God's Word has to be worked out in everyday life.

When we read the Word of God, it helps us see ourselves clearly like a mirror and the things in our lives that need to be changed. "Anyone who listens to the word but does not do what it says is like a man who looks at his face in a mirror...., but doing it....he will be blessed in what he does", James 1:23-25.

Jesus and the Holy Scriptures, the Word of God

"As the Resurrected King, God's Messiah and our Saviour, our Lord Jesus Christ has given us some of the most important statements concerning the authority and nature of the Word of God. 1) Jesus confirms the truth that every word of the Scriptures is given by God. There is no room for debate: Jesus believed and taught the plenary verbal inspiration of the Bible that every word is God-breathed (see 2 Timothy 3:16). 2) Jesus also contends that every truth the Bible teaches is to be held inviolable. In Matthew 5:17-19, He insists that everyone who teaches anything running at cross-purposes with the Scriptures is not in harmony with kingdom order. 3) Jesus attests to the indissolubility of the Scriptures (John 10:35). When He says 'the Scripture cannot be broken,' He literally describes the utter inviolability of God's Word from man's side (do not try to diminish its truth or meaning) and the utter dependability of it from God's side (He will uphold it – His Word will not dissolve or be shaken). Matthew 24:35 is the verse most quoted in this regard. All creation may dissolve: God's Word will stand forever! 4) Jesus affirms the credibility of the Old Testament in general (John 5:39), but also the miracles of the Old Testament He did not see them as superstitiously held believes, which He tolerated among those He addressed. Rather, He was the Incarnate Truth: and as the embodiment of truthfulness. His testimony is decisive. Thus, note that Jesus believed the Biblical record of: a) Adam and Eve as the first pair (Matthew 19:4-5); b) the literal destruction of Sodom and Gomorrah (Mark 6:11; Luke 17:29-30); c) the actuality of Noah and the Flood (Matthew 24:37-38); d) the trustworthiness of Daniel's prophecy (Matthew 24:15); e) the truth of Jonah's being swallowed by the great fish (Matthew 12:39-40) and f) the miracle of manna being provided, as well as other miracles during the wilderness journey of Moses' time (John 3:14; 6:31-32). Finally, 5) Jesus forecast and authorised the writing of the New Testament Scriptures in both John 14:26 and 16:12-13, He indicated that the coming ministry of the Holy Spirit would include His bringing to the apostles' mind the things that should afterward be recorded. His anticipation of that ministry not only places His endorsement upon that facet of that apostolic mission".[2]

Special Ministry of the Word of God

Knowing and obeying God's Word will bring blessings to our life. The truth of the Word of God in the heart that makes us grow in the Lord. This is well expressed in Psalm 119. What it is and what it can do in our life if we let it:

God's Word can keep us clean – We must heed God's Word (v 9) and hide God's Word in our heart (v 11).

God's Word will guide us on the pilgrim path of life – We are strangers on the earth (v 19; 1 Peter 2:11). In our Christian walk of life we need 'a road map' to help us know the way to our destination. Therefore, let us ask God to open our eyes to the Word (v 18). Let our Bible be our trusted counsellor (v 24).

God's Word brings us the blessing of life (v 25) – because it has life. "For the word of God is living and active", Hebrews 4:12a. It imparts life, "For you have been born again not of perishable seed but of imperishable, through the living and enduring word of God" (1 Peter 1:23). And it nourishes life. "Like newborn babies, crave pure spiritual milk so that by it you may grow up in your salvation", 1 Peter 2:2.

God's Word can revive and strengthen us (v 28) – even when we are in the dust. We must rejoice in God's Word, delight in it and meditate on it. There is life for us in the Word of God. Therefore, let us cultivate an appetite for the Word of God.

The Word of God will help us to make right decisions and experience right values (vv 33-37) – For many people, money is god. But far more valuable than wealth, is obedience to God because it is a heavenly treasure than earthly one (Luke 12:33). The psalmist had the right values. He would rather have God's Word than food (v 103).

Freedom is another Blessing – God will give us freedom if we love and obey His Word (v 45). His Word is truth (v 43) and 'the truth sets us free' (John 8:32). When we obey God's Word, we enjoy true freedom because His Word is 'the law of liberty' (James 2:12). Law and liberty are co-workers in our life in building character and bringing joy.

The Word of God will bring comfort to our life if we will let it (vv 49-50) – Remember God's promises (v 50) and God's name (v 55), and He will comfort us.

We will have friends who are worth having (v 63) – if we are true to God's Word. If we walk with God's people, they will help us to enjoy life and liberty.

The Word of God can encourage us in times of affliction (vv 67, 71) – When the Lord is in our mind and heart, affliction can bring out the best in us. I personally have experienced this in my affliction and suffering.

The Word of God, the Bible is God's how-to-do-it manual for making life work successfully (v 73) – It tells us how to use our body and mind, how to handle our time and money.

The Word of God will help us get victory over our enemies (vv 84-87) – When it looks like the end has come, God's Word helps us make a new beginning. (See Appendix 3: 'My Testimony').

The Word of God is settled – nothing can change it or destroy it (v 152; Matthew 24:35). "Your word, O Lord, is eternal; it stands firm in the heavens" (v 89). God is faithful and His Word can be trusted. We will have a solid foundation in a world that offers us no stability.

The Word of God give us practical wisdom (v 98) – Those of us who love God's Word and obey it develop a practical wisdom for guiding our life. Let God, not man, be our teacher (John 14:26; 16:13-15).

The Word of God is our light (v 105) – In a dark world God's Word is our light to keep us from the traps and detours of the enemy (v 110). When we cultivate a holy fear of the Lord and His Word (v 120) we will not be ashamed of our hope (v 116). God sends the light into our heart and gives us the wisdom we need. "The entrance of Your words gives light; It gives understanding to the simple", v 130 NKJV.

The Word of God will assure us – God's Word will assure us and enable us when we feel the oppression of the enemy (vv 121-122). If we love the truth, we must also hate false (v 128).

The Word of God is wonderful (v 129) – When we live by the word of God, our life becomes wonderful. The Spirit shows us wonderful things in the Word (v 18). His light shines within us (v 130) and His face shines upon us (v 135), so that we become a light in a dark world (Philippians 2:14-16).

The Word of God helps us practice righteousness in a sinful world (v 137-138) – There is no substitute for integrity, which comes from loving the Word and obeying it.

The Word of God helps us to pray in the will of God (v 145) – The better we know the Word, the more effectively we will pray (John 15:7) and the more effectively we pray, the better we learn the Word.

Knowing the Word of God and obeying it will bring joy to our hearts, the kind of joy we would have if we found a buried treasure (v 162). Along with joy, we will experience love (vv 163, 167), peace (v 165), and hope (v 166) – treasures money cannot buy.

When the Word of God fills our heart, the right words will come out of our mouth (Colossians 3:16, 4:6) and we declare God's praise unceasingly – "May my lips over flow with praise, for you teach me your decrees. May my tongue sing of your word, for all your commands are righteous. Let me live that I may praise you, and may your laws sustain me" (vv 71-72, 175).

Our Relationship to the Word of God: Esteem His Word

Let us now discover what we must do with God's Word (Psalm 119):

We must love it, not just read it – "Oh, how I love your law! And meditate on it all day long", v 97.

We must treasure it – "The law from your mouth is more precious to me than thousands of pieces of silver and gold", v 72.

We must learn it – "I recounted my ways and you answered me; teach me your decrees. Let me understand the teachings of your precepts; then I will meditate on your wonders", vv 26-27.

We must memorise it – "I have hidden your word in my heart that I might not sin against you", v 11.

We must meditate on it – "I meditate on your precepts and consider your ways", v 15; (see also Psalm 1:2-3; Joshua 1:8).

We must delight in it – "Your statutes are my delight; they are my counsellors", v 24. "But his delight is in the law of the Lord ...", Psalm 1:2a, thus he is blessed.

We must believe it – "Then I will answer the one who taunts me, for I trust in your word", v 42; (see Hebrews 4:2; Romans 10:17).

We must study it and know it – "Do your best to present yourself to God as one approved, a workman who does not need to be ashamed and who correctly handles the word of truth", 2 Timothy 2:15.

We must practice it – "Blessed....who walk according to the law of the LORD. Blessed are they who keep his statutes...., they walk in his ways....that are to be fully obeyed", vv 1-4; (see James 1:23-25).

We must speak it – "It is written: 'I believed; therefore I have spoken'. With that same spirit of faith we also believe and therefore speak", 2 Corinthians 4:13.

We must confess it – "That if you confess with your mouth 'Jesus is Lord', and believe in your heart that God raised him from the dead you will be saved. For it is with your heart that you believe and are justified, and it is with your mouth that you confess and are saved", Romans 10:9-10; (see also Mark 11:23-24).

Concluding Remarks

God reveals Himself in the Scriptures (Psalm 19:7-11). Verses 7-11 tell us what the Bible can do for us if only we will read it, meditate on it, and obey it. In this Psalm, David expresses the great desire of his heart, "May the words of my mouth and the meditation of my heart be pleasing in your sight, O LORD, my Rock and my Redeemer", v 14.

The Psalms tell of the road to success. Everyone wants to prosper. No one wishes to fail. The psalmist says that every one may prosper, and the things to do are read the Bible, delight in it and meditate upon it (Psalm 1:2-3). "Do not let this Book of the Law depart from your mouth; meditate on it day and night, so that you may be careful to do everything written in it. Then you will be prosperous and successful", Joshua 1:8.

Finally, we have to allow the Holy Spirit to guide our lives with the Word; He is called the 'Spirit of Truth' (John 16:13) and He works with 'the Word of Truth'. "Do your best to present yourself to God as one approved, a workman who does not need to be ashamed and who correctly handles the word of truth', 2 Timothy 2:15. Yes, God is still speaking to us through His written Word and through the voice of the Holy Spirit.

(Please read Appendix 1: 'The Role of the Bible in Embracing Life to the Full').

Chapter 14

POWER OF PRAYER

If any of you lacks wisdom, he should ask God,
who gives generously to all without finding fault,
and it will be given to him (James 1:5)

Introduction

Prayer is a conversation with God – in praise, thanksgiving, petition or intercession. Prayer is a command of God. "Call to me and I will answer you and tell you great and unsearchable things you do not know", Jeremiah 33:3. Our loving Father invites us to pray to Him because God loves us. "...God demonstrates his own love for us in this: While we were still sinners, Christ died for us", Romans 5:8. God wants us to pray and seek Him so He can show Himself to us as Jehovah Jireh, so we will know Him to be our provider. In both Matthew 7:7-12 and Luke 11:9-10, Jesus told us to "ask and receive". Jesus encourages us to ask and to receive (Matthew 7:7; Mark 11:24). Prayer should be an integral part of our lives, not just practiced in emergencies. Make talking to God a habit. Tell Him about anything, anytime, and anywhere (Psalm 34:6). Roy Warren says, "Prayer is the vehicle by which we enter the battle; the word of God is our weapon in the battle".

Why We Need to Pray

Jesus is in heaven now. But one day He will come back to rule on the earth and all the kingdoms of the earth will be the kingdoms of our Lord Jesus Christ (Revelation 11:15). But today, in the day of salvation and grace, He extends His kingdom rule in the hearts of people who respond willingly to the gospel and make Him the Lord of their lives (Romans 10:9-10; Matthew 11:12). He reigns on High and we are seated with Him (Ephesians 2:6). And He exercises His authority on earth through His body, the church (Matthew 28:18-20). As the Body of Christ on the earth today we extend His kingdom influence as we do the same things He did (John 14:12) through prayer to the Father for His kingdom to come and His will be done.

The Bible says that He has made us to be a kings and priests to our God (Revelation 1:6, 5:10; 1 Peter 2:5, 9). As priests represent the people to God – we do that through prayer and intercession. Our prayers as God's representative people on earth give God legal access to act on earth. It seems that God can only or largely act on earth by permission or invitation! So when we pray we are setting in motion the activity of God in the heavens and on the earth, to bring about His will and the extension of the kingly rule of Christ upon the earth. In other words, prayer that is based on the completed work of Christ makes a huge difference.

We Are Commanded to Pray

The Bible says, "Look to the LORD and his strength; seek his face always", 1 Chronicles 16:11; "Ask and it will be given to you; seek and you will find; knock and the door will be open to you", Matthew 7:7. Let us remember to ask, seek, and knock as our Lord commanded us to do; "Watch and pray so that you will not fall into temptation", Matthew 26:41. Jesus said, "they should always pray and not give up", Luke 18:1. We must persevere in prayer. As we persistent in prayer we grow in character, faith and hope. "Until now you have not asked for anything in my name. Ask and you will receive, and your joy will be complete", John 16:24; "And pray in the Spirit on all occasions with all kinds of prayers and requests", Ephesians 6:18a.

Biblical Basis for Effective Prayer

Pray by the guidance of the Holy Spirit – "...the spirit helps us in our weakness. We do not know what we ought to pray for, but the Spirit himself intercedes for us with groans that words cannot express. And he who searches our hearts knows the mind of the Spirit,.... in accordance with God's will", Romans 8:26-27.

Pray with a clean heart and right motive – Holiness is essential (1 Peter 1:16-17). Pray, "Search me, O God and know my heart; test me and know my anxious thoughts. See if there is any offensive way in me, and lead me in the way everlasting", Psalm 139:23-24; "When you ask, you do not receive, because you ask with wrong motives ...", James 4:3.

Pray in faith (believing) – "If you believe, you will receive whatever you ask for in prayer", Matthew 21:22. We must believe that He will perform it (Hebrews 11:6). The Bible says in Mark 11, "Have faith in God ...", v 22 and "...whatever you ask in prayer, believe that you have received it, and it will be yours", v 24.

Pray wholeheartedly – It is important that we seek Him diligently. "...you will call upon me and come and pray to me, and I will listen to you. You will seek me and find me when you seek me with all your heart. I will be found by you...", Jeremiah 29:12-14.

Pray in obedience to the Word of God – "If you remain in me and my words remain in you, ask whatever you wish and it will be given you", John 15:7; "...receive from him anything we ask, because we obey his commands and do what pleases him", 1 John 3:22. (Note: Remaining in Christ means – believing that he is God's Son, 1 John 4:15); receiving him as Saviour and Lord (John 1:12); doing what God says (1 John 3:24); continuing to believe the gospel (1 John 2:24); and relating in love to the community of believers, Christ's body (John 15:12).

Pray according to His will – "This is the confidence we have in approaching God: that if we ask anything according to his will, he hears us", 1 John 5:14; "receive from him anything we ask, because we obey his commands and do what pleases him", 1 John 3:22.

Pray in His name – There is power in the name of Jesus. To pray in the name of Jesus is 'to pray in the mind and spirit of Jesus, while we believe His promises, rely upon His grace, and work' because Jesus has unlimited credit in heaven. "And I will do whatever you ask in my name, so that the Son may bring glory to the Father. You may ask me for in anything in my name, and I will do it", John 14:13-14.

Pray with another believer – In the body of believers (the church), the sincere agreement of two people especially with relevant Scripture is very powerful. "...I tell you that if two of you on earth agree about anything you ask for, it will be done for you by my Father in heaven", Matthew 18:19.

Be joyful and thankful – "Be joyful always; pray continually; give thanks in all circumstances, for this is God's will for you in Christ Jesus", 1 Thessalonians 5:16-18; "Rejoice in the Lord always...", "... in everything, by prayer and petition, with thanksgiving, present your requests to God", Philippians 4:4,6.

Pray with a forgiving heart – Forgiveness is essential. "And when you stand praying, if you hold anything against anyone forgive him, so that your Father in heaven may forgive your sins", Mark 11:25.

Pray with a right attitude – "The prayer of a righteous man is powerful and effective", James 5:16; "Elijah was a man just like us. He prayed earnestly that it would not rain, and it did not rain for three and a half years", James 5:17; (see also v 18).

Pray with a contrite heart – Prayer is blocked by sin. "If my people who are called by my name, will humble themselves and pray and seek my face and turn from their wicked ways, then will I hear from heaven and will forgive their sin and will heal their land", 2 Chronicles 7:14; "The sacrifices of God are a broken spirit; a broken and contrite heart, ...", Psalm 51:17.

Prayer is blocked by mistreating our spouse – "Husbands, in the same way be considerate as you live with your wives, and treat them with respect as the weaker partner and as heirs with you of the gracious gift of life, so that nothing will hinder your prayers", 1 Peter 3:7.

Love and right relationships are essential – Love and right relationships with one another is important to God (1 John 2:10). The sacrifice Jesus made not only sets our relationship right with God but should help us set our relationships right with one another (Ephesians 2:14-18).

Jesus Teaches Us about Prayer

Jesus gave instructions where, how and what to pray (Matthew 6:5-15). Our public praying is only as good as our private praying, and our private praying should be secret (vv 5-6), sincere (vv 7-8) and to some extent systematic (vv 9-13). The Lord's Prayer is a pattern for us to follow so that we will put God's concern first and to not forget to forgive others: "Our Father in heaven, hallowed be your name, your kingdom come, your will be done on earth as it is in heaven. Give us today our daily bread. Forgive us our debts, as we also have forgiven our debtors. And lead us not into temptation, but deliver us from the evil one", Matthew 9b-13.

Jesus Teaches Us about Asking, Seeking, Knocking (Matthew 7:7-12)

Jesus tells us to persist in pursuing God. Knowing God takes faith, focus, and follow-through, and Jesus assures us that we will be rewarded. Let us not give up in our efforts to seek God. Let us also learn to ask for what is good for us, and then he grants it. God is a loving Father who understands, cares and comforts. If humans can be kind, imagine how kind God, the Creator can be. "Ask and it will be given to you; seek and you will find; knock and the door will be open to you. For everyone who asks receives; he who seeks finds; and to him who knocks, the door will be opened", Matthew 7:7-8.

God Is a Prayer-hearing God and a Prayer-answering God

God will answer our earnest prayers. We note in 2 Chronicles 6:19-42 that Solomon led the people in prayer, he asked God to hear their prayers concerning a variety of their situations such as, crime, vv 22-23; enemy attacks, vv 24-25; drought, vv 26-27; famine, vv 28-31; influx of foreigners, vv 32-33; war, vv 34-35; sin, vv 36-39. God answered Solomon's prayer with four conditions in 2 Chronicles 7:14 for forgiveness: humble yourself by admitting; pray to God, asking forgiveness; seek God continually, and turn from sinful behaviour.

God is concerned with whatever we face, even the difficult consequences we bring upon ourselves. He wants us to turn to Him in prayer. When we pray, let us remember that God hears us. Don't allow the extremity of our situation cause us to doubt His care for us. Hannah said in 1 Samuel 1:27 "I prayed for this child, and the LORD has granted me what I asked of him".

How Can We Hear God

God wants to speak to us. In the past God spoke through the prophets. Today He is speaking even more precisely especially through His Son (Hebrews 1:1-2). In Acts chapter 10, we notice that God speaks clearly, powerfully, over and over again unmistakable way. Cornelius prayed. He had a life of prayer. He prayed regularly (v 2). Peter went up to the roof top to pray (v 9). Our God is a God who speaks. The Christian faith is the only faith that has a God who speaks. He is speaking to our lives day after day. Jesus said, "When you pray, go into your room, close the door and pray to your Father, who is unseen. Then your Father, who sees what is done in secret, will reward you", Matthew 6:6.

Praying in His Will

There are two prayers written by the apostle Paul in Ephesians complement each other and help us pray about the will of God for our lives. Ephesians 1:15-23 focus on knowing what God has done for us in Christ. Paul prayed that the Ephesians would know Christ better because Christ is our model. It is for enlightenment. While chapter 3:14-21 emphasize experiencing God's blessings. It is for enablement. We must appropriate that fullness through faith and prayer as we daily live for Him.

The other prison prayers of Paul are recorded in Philippians 1:9-11 and Colossians 1:9-12. Paul's prayer to the Philippians was that they would be unified in love and would discern what is best. Paul's prayer pattern for the Colossians teach us how to pray for others: understand God's will, gain spiritual wisdom, please and honour God, bear good fruit, grow in the knowledge of God, be filled with God's strength, have great endurance and patience, stay full of Christ's joy, and give thanks always. Paul's prayers are also for us and the church. Therefore, we may use these prayers for ourselves and know that we are praying in the will of God.

Intercession

Intercession means praying to God for someone else or to bring about changes in some things or situations. Some examples of intercessory prayers are found in the Bible: Abraham intercedes for Sodom (Genesis 18:16-33); Moses intercedes for Israel after the golden calf (Exodus 32:1-14 and Deuteronomy 9:7-19); Moses intercedes for Israel after the refusal to enter the Promised Land (Numbers 14:1-20 and Deuteronomy 9:23-29); Hezekiah intercedes for Jerusalem in the face of attack (2 Kings 19:9-37); Ezra intercedes for the returned exiles to Jerusalem following intermarriage (Ezra 9:1-10,17); Nehemiah intercedes for Jerusalem in disrepair (Nehemiah 1:1-2:9); Daniel intercedes for the exiles to return to Jerusalem (Daniel 9:1-23); The apostles and believers intercede in the face of opposition to the gospel (Acts 4:23-31).

Praying for others

The way is to pray that we may be right and a blessing to others. To quote F. E. Marsh (*1000 Bible Study Outlines*), "Two young people, a boy and girl aged six and eight, were being put to bed by their mother, and she, like a good mother, saw that they prayed before they got into bed, but just before she had taken them to the bedroom, the boy had provoked his mother and she had spoken to him reprovingly. When the boy was saying his prayers, he said, 'Oh Lord, bless Mamma, and save her from getting cross'. When the girl prayed, she prayed more consistently; she implored the Lord to 'Bless Mamma, and save us from making her cross'"[1].

God at the centre of intercession

Intercession is all about God. God is at the centre of all life and particularly the Christian life. The reason we intercede is because Jesus is interceding. The reason we intercede is to give God what He wants. The heart of intercession is – "Let Your kingdom come, let Your will be done". We are seeking first and foremost to identify God's will through prayer and his Word and then to pray and intercede that into being. The wonderful intercessory prayer as recorded in John 17 is a sample of how the Lord is interceding for His people now.

Fasting with Prayer

Fasting usually involves missing food in order to humble ourselves and draw near to God in prayer. The main motivation of setting aside food for a time is in order to draw near to God in prayer (Matthew 17:21, 1 Corinthians 7:5). Let us look at some reasons people fasted in the New Testament: to pray and send people out into ministry (Acts 13:2); Jesus fasted before beginning His ministry (Matthew 4:2); to deal with the unbelief that prevents souls being set free from the bondage of evil (Matthew 17:14-21). Some examples in the Old Testament include: to humble one's soul before God (Ezra 8:21); to mourn over personal sin and failure (1 Samuel 7:6); to mourn over the sins of the church, nation, and world (1 Samuel 7:3-6); to show repentance (2 Samuel 12:16); to gain revelation, wisdom, and understanding concerning the will of God (Daniel 9:3,21-22); to discipline the body for self-control (Psalm 35:13).

How Fasting Helps

Fasting humbles our soul and allows the grace of God to flow. Fasting subdues our flesh, and quickens our spiritual man. Therefore, fasting, rightly practiced, brings both our soul and our body into subjection to the Holy Spirit. Fasting changes us such that God's power can flow through us more effectively to bring about His purposes through our prayers, words and actions.

Prayer example of Jesus

We see the example of prayer and intercession so well in the life and ministry of Jesus. Jesus received the baptism in the Holy Spirit while in prayer after his water baptism (Luke 3:21-22); Jesus launched into his ministry after prayer and fasting (Luke 4:1-14); Jesus gained direction in his ministry following prayer with the Father (Mark 1:35-39); Jesus prayed before he called His twelve disciples (Luke 6:12-13); Jesus prayed for labourers in the harvest field, before sending his twelve disciples out into the harvest field (Matthew

9:35-38, 10:1-8); Jesus interceded for his disciples in prayer, for their protection, unity, holiness and success in the ministry (John 17); Jesus prayed for those whom his disciples would win (John 17:20); Jesus prayed for help for Peter, that his faith wouldn't fail him and although he failed initially, he subsequently went on to be a foundational leader in the early church (Luke 22:31-32).

Concluding Remarks

The Bible is full of examples of those who saw great results from crying out to God in prayer. History is also full of examples of men and women who took God at His word and shaped their world through intercession. One of the most powerful men of prayer in the Christian church was George Mueller. He housed, clothed and fed thousands of orphans solely through prayer. He provided financial support to the ministry of Hudson Taylor through the means of prayer. Mueller once stated that he believed that God had given him more than thirty thousand souls in answer to prayer.

Prayer should be motivated by love; fervent (from the heart); based on the Word of God; led by the Spirit of God; done believing that God hears us; done believing that God answers us; done in faith, receiving what we ask for; done with thanksgiving because we have it; prayed to the Father in the name of Jesus.

Pray and act with great confidence in accordance with God's Word and by the leading of the Holy Spirit knowing that Jesus has wonderfully regained all authority and power and seeks to exercise it through His church – we are His mouth, His hands and His feet on earth today. Prayer preceded Pentecost, and helped continue in the ministry of the Spirit. Where prayer is lacking in a church it will soon die of dry rot. Mathew Henry says, 'Prayer is the key of the morning and the lock of the evening'. 'Prayer is a mighty instrument, not for getting man's will done in heaven, but for getting God's will done in earth' (Robert Law).

Let us conclude this study with the words of Joseph M. Scriven, 'What a friend we have in Jesus, All our sins and grieves to bear! What a privilege to carry, Everything to God in prayer!'

Chapter 15

THANKSGIVING, PRAISE AND WORSHIP

Everything on earth will worship you; they will sing your praises,
shouting your name in glorious songs. (Psalm 66:4 NLT)

Introduction

Worship starts by thinking about God. It is thinking about 'the Creator and giver of all that is good'. Our very first thoughts about God should be one of gratitude. Accordingly, worship begins by saying thank you! It begins by thanking God for the very precious gift of life. When we look around at the wonder of everything God has made thanksgiving, gratitude and praise should be our response. Wrapped up in creation is God's eternal love and grace. Every day, each breath we breathe is a gift from a loving God.

Derek Prince says, "Three activities of human spirit – thanks giving, praise and worship – enable us to relate to three different aspects of God's nature. By thanksgiving for all the kind, good things He does for us, we acknowledge God's goodness. By praise

– our appropriate response to His awe-inspiring majesty – we acknowledge God's greatness. And by worship we acknowledge God's holiness"[1].

Thanksgiving

Thanksgiving is to acknowledge God's goodness. It describes what God has done rather than what He is. Giving thanks is not an option. It is a command. Be thankful (Colossians 3:15). Thankfulness provides access to God. There are two stages to access God – "into His gates with thanksgiving, and into His courts with praise", Psalm 100:4. It unlocks the supernatural miracle power of God. For example, 'Jesus feeds the five thousand'. In all that we do we need to be guided by two principles: doing it 'in the name of the Lord Jesus' and 'giving thanks to God through Him' (Colossians 3:16-17).

The importance and spiritual benefits of thanksgiving in our prayer life cannot be overemphasized. The Bible tells us God resists the proud but gives grace to the humble (James 4:6). How do we become humble? It is done by being thankful! A good rule is to be anxious for nothing (Philippians 4:6), be prayerful in all things, and be thankful for everything (1 Thessalonians 5:18).

Two main things we are to thank God for:

To thank Him for His work in creation (see Psalm 100) – God alone is worthy of being worshipped. This psalm tells us to remember God's goodness and dependability, and then to worship with thanksgiving and praise (v 4). "Know that the LORD, He is God; It is He who has made us, and not we ourselves; We are His people and the sheep of His pasture", v 3 NKJV. In Revelation 4:11, we read, "You are worthy, O Lord, to receive glory and honour and power; For You created all things, And by Your will they exist and were created", NKJV.

To thank Him for His work in redemption – "And they sang a new song: 'You are worthy to take the scroll and to open its seals, because You were slain, and with your blood you purchased men for God from every tribe and language and people and nation'", Revelation 5:9.

Some other areas for thanksgiving:

"Give thanks in all circumstances for this is God's will for you in Christ Jesus", (1 Thessalonians 5:18).

"Enter his gates with thanksgiving and his courts with praise; give thanks to him and praise his name" (Psalm 100:4)Thank the Lord for His message (Acts 13:48).

Thank the Lord for all believers (Romans 1:8).

Thank God for His Son for His 'indescribable gift' (2 Corinthians 9:15).

Give thanks to God for everything (Ephesians 5:20).

Always thank the Father (Colossians 1:12-14).

Every time a person ceases to be thankful he or she starts down to a slippery path (Romans 1:21; 2 Timothy 3:2).

Praise

To praise God is to acknowledge the glories of His excellent person. Praise is expressing to God our appreciation and understanding of His worth. It is saying 'thank you' for each aspect of His divine nature. "I will praise you, O Lord, with all my heart; I will tell of all your wonders", Psalm 9:1. Psalm 8 declares the majesty of God, He, the Creator of all the heavens, the moon, and stars; is truly majestic and worthy of praise, honour, and worship (vv 1, 3-4).

Some facts about praise:

God alone is worthy of our praise (Psalm 188:3; 113:3).

It is His will for us that we will praise Him (Psalm 50:23).

Praising God should be continuous (Psalm 34:1, 71:6).

We are to praise God for His holiness (2 Chronicles 20:21).

All nature praises God (Psalm 148:7-10).

The sun, moon, and stars praise Him (Psalm 19:1, 143:3).

The angels praise Him (Psalm 148:2).

Praise prepares the way for God's supernatural intervention (Psalm 50:23).

Praise pleases God and beautifies God's people (Psalm 149:4, 147:1-11).

How should we praise God?

With our whole heart (Psalm 111:1), with understanding (Psalm 47:7), with lifted hands – joyful mouth and lips (Psalm 63:4-5), lifting the hands – like an evening sacrifice (Psalm 141:2), with the dance (Psalm 149:3), with the tambourine and dance (Psalm 150:4).

When and why should we praise God?

We should praise God every day, forever and ever, at all times and continually.

The book of Psalms has a vast number of praise psalms that end with praises offered to the Lord who had done so much for His people.

For example, Psalm 104 praises God for His fullness as Creator; Psalm 105, for His faithfulness as Redeemer, and Psalm 106 for His forgiveness as Saviour of His people.

The final Psalm (150) invites us all to praise the Lord. The word 'praise' is used thirteen times in this psalm. This psalm tells us where, why, how and who should praise Him:

Where should we praise Him? – Wherever we are, praise the Lord (v 1).

Why should we praise Him? – Because of what He does and who He is (v 2).

How should we praise Him? – With voices and instruments (vv 3-5).

Who should praise Him? – Everything that has breath. (v 6). Our breath comes from Him (Acts 17:25). So we ought to use it to praise His name.

All creation, and the whole universe, are called upon to praise the Creator, Sustainer and Redeemer of every living and inanimate thing!

Worship

Worship is an appropriate response to God's self-revelation. Worship refers to the supreme honour or veneration given either in thought or deed to a person or thing. Worship is one of the main themes of the Bible and that is of tremendous importance, for effective worship belongs only to God. The act of worship is the supreme way by which we acknowledge that He is our God (Psalm 95:6). The Bible teaches that God alone is worthy of worship. God Almighty alone is worthy of worship. True worship is a total commitment of our body, mind, and spirit. It is about exalting, adoring and acknowledging the God of the Bible. To worship God is to express our love, affection and awe of who He is.

True worship involves at least three important elements:

It requires reverence – This includes the honour and respect directed toward the Lord in thought and feeling. Jesus said that those who worship God must do so 'in spirit and truth' (John 4:24).

It includes public expression – we express our thanks publically with a thank-offering (Leviticus 7:12).

It means service – worship especially includes the joyful service which Christians render to God. The concept of worship must not be restricted to church attendance, but should embrace an entire life of obedience to God. We can worship God in church, in the garden, while we are shopping or in the shower.

The Expressions of Worship

Worship especially includes praise and thanksgiving which may be expressed privately or publically. The Bible says in Hebrews, "Through Jesus, therefore let us continually offer to God a sacrifice of praise – the fruit of lips that confess his name", 13:15; and "Therefore, since we are receiving a kingdom that cannot be shaken, let us be thankful, and so worship God acceptably with reverence and awe, for our 'God is a consuming fire'", Hebrews 12:29.

We can worship God through prayer, singing, raising our hands in adoration, dance, playing instruments and using flags and banners. "Let the whole earth sing to the Lord! Each day proclaim the good news that he saves. Publish his glorious deeds among the nations. Tell everyone about the amazing things he does. Great is the Lord! He is most worthy of praise. He is to be feared above all gods. The gods of other nations are mere idols, but the Lord made the heavens! Honour and majesty surround him; strength and joy fill his dwelling. O nations of the world recognise the Lord, recognise that the Lord is glorious and strong. Give to the Lord the glory he deserves! Bring your offering and come to worship him. Worship the Lord in all his holy splendour", 1 Chronicles 16:25-29 NLT.

One very important expression of worship for the church is remembering the death of Christ through the Lord's Supper. The Lord's Supper was instituted by Christ Himself (see chapter 17: The Lord's Supper).

Since worship means giving something to God, the cheerful giving of money to God's work is certainly an act of worship.

The giving of one's time to the Lord is considered as worship unto Him. In fact, life should be an act of worship in obedience to God, devotion to God, faithful and joyous service to God.

The Reasons for Worship

God commands His people to worship Him – The first four of the Ten Commandments, clearly charge men to worship the one true God and Him alone (Exodus 20:3-10). We are destined to pay homage to God.

God deserves our worship – He alone possesses attributes that merit our worship and service. For example, God's goodness, mercy, holiness and creative power. When we experience the glory of God, we cannot help but fall prostrate in worship.

We need to release our worship to our Creator for personal fulfilment and joyful satisfaction for the present (Romans 12:2) and participate in the occupation of heaven (Revelation 7:9-12).

Concluding Remarks

God is holy, righteous, and a loving Father, and he is worthy of our praise and worship. The Bible tells us in Deuteronomy 6:5, to "Love the Lord your God with all your heart and with all your soul and with all your strength". Jesus said, "Yet a time is coming and has now come when the true worshippers will worship the Father in spirit and truth, for they are the kind of worshippers the Father seeks. God is spirit, and his worshippers must worship in spirit and in truth", John 4:23-24.

Our praise should come from the Holy Spirit within (Ephesians 5:18-20) and be based on Scripture (Colossians 3:16). In this way, we worship Him 'in spirit and truth'. We worship Him because of who God is and what God does. The better we know God, the more we will worship Him. The more we experience His grace in daily life, the more praise we will bring to Him.

In all ages and every culture there is a longing for worship in the heart of man. According to the New Testament, the church is the Body of Christ where God inhabits the praises of His people. His glory, His power, His great works, His wonders and His holiness make Him worthy of our worship.

Let us take time to ponder the progression: Thanksgiving leads to praise; Praise energises us to worship and that in turn causes us in union with God.

Chapter 16

WHO AM I IN CHRIST

Then you will know the truth, and the truth will set you free.
(John 8:32)

Introduction

God said that he will do 'a new thing' in the lives of his people. God provided redemption for all mankind; redemption from sin, poverty, sickness and spiritual death. All things have been dealt with through the power of the gospel and the death, burial and resurrection of Christ. When we study the scriptures we will find the message of who we are, what we are, where we are and what we have in Christ Jesus. We have a brand-new identity in Christ.

Our True Identity in Christ

We are justified – Declared 'not guilty' of sin (Romans 3:24).

No condemnation awaits us – Thank God, He has declared us not guilty and has offered us freedom from sin and power to do His will (Romans 8:1).

We are set free from the law of sin and death – "because through Christ Jesus the law of the Spirit of life set me free", Romans 8:2. This spirit of life is the Holy Spirit. The Holy Spirit gives us the power we need to live life to the full.

We are sanctified and made acceptable in Jesus Christ – (1 Corinthians 1:2). Sanctified means, that we are chosen or set apart by Christ for His service. We are 'called to be holy'.

We are righteous and holy in Christ – "It is because of him that you are in Christ Jesus, who has become for us wisdom from God – that is, our righteousness, holiness and redemption", 1 Corinthians 1:30.

We will be made alive at the resurrection – "For as in Adam all died, so in Christ all will be made alive", 1 Corinthians 15:22.

We are a new creation – We are re-created (new creations), living in vital union with Christ (2 Corinthians 5:17).

We receive God's righteousness – Our sin was poured into Christ at His crucifixion. His righteousness is poured into us at our conversion (2 Corinthians 5:21).

We are one in Christ with all other believers – "...for you are all one in Christ Jesus", Galatians 3:28. No one is more privileged than or superior to any one else.

We are blessed with every spiritual blessing in Christ – It means that in Christ we have all the benefits of knowing God (Ephesians 1:3).

We are holy, blameless and covered with God's love – Because of Christ we are holy and blameless in God's sight (Ephesians 1:4).

We are adopted as God's children in His infinite love – God graciously accepts us now that we belong to His dear Son (Ephesians 1:5-6).

Our sins are taken away and we are forgiven – We are forgiven on the basis of the shedding of Jesus' blood – He died as the perfect and final sacrifice (Ephesians 1:7).

We will be brought under Christ's headship – All people will bow to Jesus as Lord either because they love Him or because they fear His power (Ephesians 1:10-11).

We are marked as belonging to God by the Holy Spirit – The presence of the Holy Spirit in us demonstrates the genuineness of our faith, proves that we are God's children (Ephesians 1:13).

We have been raised up to sit with Christ in glory – Our eternal life with Christ is certain because we are united in His powerful victory (Ephesians 2:6).

We are God's work of art – God's workmanship and masterpiece (Ephesians 2:10). Our salvation is something only God can do. It is His powerful, creative work in us.

We have been brought near to God – "...in Christ Jesus you who once were far away have been brought near through the blood of Christ (Ephesians 2:13). Only Christ breaks down the walls of prejudice, reconciles all believers to God, and unifies us in one body. Let us humbly thank God for what He has done.

We share in the promise in Christ – "...through the gospel the Gentiles are heirs together ... and sharers together in the promise in Christ Jesus", Ephesians 3:6.

We can come with freedom and confidence into God's presence – With thanks to Christ, by faith we can enter directly into God's presence through prayer (Ephesians 3:12). This is an awesome privilege.

We are members of Christ's body, the church – Christ is the head of His church and we are the body (Ephesians 5:29-30).

We have been given fullness in Christ – Christ alone holds the answers to the true meaning of life because He is life (Colossians 2:10).

We are set free from our sinful nature – Christ sets us free from our evil desires by a spiritual operation, not a bodily one. God removes the old nature and gives us a nature (Colossians 2:11).

We will have eternal glory – "...may obtain the salvation that is in Christ Jesus, with eternal glory", 2 Timothy 2:10.

I am accepted in Christ

I am God's child – All who welcome Jesus Christ as Lord of their lives are reborn spiritually, receiving new life from God (John 1:12).

I am Christ's friend – How comforting and reassuring to be chosen as Christ's friend and yet Jesus Christ is Lord and Master (John 15:15).

I have been justified – We enjoy the peace that comes from being made right with God (Romans 5:1).

I am united with Christ – "But he who unites himself with the Lord is one with Him in spirit", 1 Corinthians 6:17. We as Christians are free to be all we can be for God, but we are not free from God.

I have been bought by Christ – Christ's death freed us from sin, but also obligates us to His service – "You were bought at a price", 1 Corinthians 6:20.

I am a member of His Body – "Now you are the Body of Christ ..." 1 Corinthians 12:27.

I am one of His saints – "To the saints in Ephesus, the faithful in Christ Jesus", Ephesians 1:1.

He has adopted me – God has adopted us as His own children.

Through Jesus' sacrifice, He has brought us into his family and made us heirs along with Jesus (Ephesians 1:5).

I have direct access to God – All are now free to come to God through Christ – "access to the Father by one Spirit", Ephesians 2:18.

I have been redeemed, my sins are forgiven – Jesus bought our freedom from sin and judgement. He forgave all our sins (Colossians 1:14).

I am complete in Christ – No Christians needs anything in addition to that which Christ has provided to be saved. Christ alone holds the answers to the true meaning of life, because He is life (Colossians 2:10).

I am secure in Christ

I am free for ever from condemnation – "Therefore, there is now no condemnation for those who are in Christ Jesus", Romans 8:1. The verdict is 'not guilty'.

I am assured all things work together for the good – God works in 'all things'. This promise is for all those who love God (Romans 8:28).

I am free from any condemning charges – God has acquitted us and removed our sin and guilt, so it is Satan who accuses us (Romans 8:33-34).

I cannot be separated from the love of God – "Who shall separate us from the love of Christ?", Romans 8:35. God tells us how great His love is, so that we will totally secure in him.

I have been established in Christ – "Now it is God who makes both us and you stand firm in Christ. He anointed us, set his seal of ownership on us", 2 Corinthians 1:21-22. The Holy Spirit, who guarantees that we belong to him.

I am hidden with Christ in God – The believer's life is concealed and safe in Him (Colossians 3:3).

I am confident the good work begun in me will be perfected – The Holy Spirit lives in us, enabling us to be more like Christ every day. God promises to finish the work he has begun (Philippians 1:6).

I am a citizen of heaven – because we belong to Christ (Philippians 3:20).

I have not been given a spirit of fear – The power of the Holy Spirit can help us overcome our fear of what some might say or do to us, so that we can continue to do God's work in love and self-discipline (2 Timothy 1:7).

I can find grace and mercy to help in time of need – Let us come with reverence as well as bold assurance because he is our King, Friend and Counsellor (Hebrews 4:16).

I am born of God and the evil one cannot harm me – God keeps us safe from Satan's schemes because we belong to Him and obey him (1 John 5:18).

I am significant in Christ

I am the salt of the earth and light of the world – We are called to be the salt of the earth as seasoning brings out the best flavour in food. We are called to be a beacon of truth (light). If we live for Christ, we will glow like lights, showing others what Christ is like (Matthew 5:13-14).

I am a branch of the true vine – The branches are all those who claim to be followers of Christ and produce much fruit (John 15:1, 5).

I have been chosen and appointed to bear fruit – fruit that will last – and to live with him forever (John 15:16).

I am a personal witness of Christ – We should show and tell others what God has done for us (Acts 1:8).

I am God's temple – "Don't you know that you yourselves are God's temple and that God's Spirit lives in you?", 1 Corinthians 3:16.

I am a minister of reconciliation – Because we have been reconciled to God, we have the privilege of encouraging others to do the same; and thus we are those who have the 'ministry of reconciliation' (2 Corinthians 5:18-20).

I am God's co-worker – "As God's fellow workers we urge you not to receive God's grace in vain", 2 Corinthians 6:1.

I am seated with Christ in the heavenly realm – Our eternal life with Christ is certain because we are united in His powerful victory (Ephesians 2:6).

I am God's workmanship – Our salvation is something only God can do. It is his powerful creative work in us (Ephesians 2:10).

I may approach God with freedom and confidence – Thanks to Christ, by faith we can enter directly into God's presence through prayer. We can converse with him about everything. It is an awesome privilege (Ephesians 3:12).

I can do all things through Christ who strengthens me – The power we receive in union with Christ is sufficient to do his will and overcome challenges (Philippians 4:13).

Power of Confession

The Word of God reveals that born-again believers are new creatures in Christ Jesus (2 Corinthians 5:17) with eternal life and the very nature of God (1 John 5:10-13). And as believers we have been delivered out of Satan's power and translated into God's kingdom (Colossians 1:12-14). Speaking things out is an essential part of how we get victory. There is great power and victory in speaking out the truth – especially the truth of who God is, what his will is and what he is doing.

Our confessions rule us

'A spiritual law that few people realize is that our confessions rule us! We will never rise above our confession – saved or unsaved. In Mark 11:23, Jesus tells us that we can have any thing we say as long as we do not doubt in our heart (spirit) but believe in our heart and confess it with our mouth. Many people have a lot of head knowledge of the Bible. That in itself is not enough. But we need to obey God's Word, for example for salvation as described in Romans 10:9-10 "that if you confess with your mouth, "Jesus is Lord", and believe in your heart that God raised him from the dead, you will be saved. For it is with your heart that you believe and are justified, and it is with your mouth that you confess and are saved". The law of confession works for everything in life including healing (Matthew 8:17; Isaiah 53:4; 1 Peter 2:24)'.[1]

"Therefore, holy brethren, partakers of a heavenly calling, consider Jesus, the Apostle and High priest of our confession", Hebrews 3:1 NKJV. Jesus is called here the 'High priest of our confession'. A High priest goes before God to represent the people to God and to pray for them. Jesus is the High Priest of our confession. Speaking out what the Bible says has to be the greatest confession we can ever make. "Also I say to you, everyone who confesses Me before men, him the Son of Man will confess also before the angels of God", Luke 12:8 NKJV.

We need to believe what God says in his Word regardless of how we feel about ourselves. Let us begin to personalise God's Word, confess it daily with our mouth, believe it in our heart and begin to act upon it until it becomes a reality. For example:

God always causes me to triumph in Christ (2 Corinthians 2:14).

God always causes me to have victory in Christ therefore I stand firm and let nothing move me (1 Corinthians 15:57).

I resist the devil and he flees from me (James 4:7).

I can do all things in Christ who strengthens me (Philippians 4:13).

I am more than a conqueror (Romans 8:37).

I am an overcomer in all things (John 16:33).

Because I am born of God I overcome the world by faith (1 John 5:4).

I have power to tread and trample on snakes and scorpions and over all the power of the enemy and nothing by any means shall harm me (Luke 10:19).

Whatever I bind on earth will be bound in heaven; whatever I loose on earth will be loosed in heaven (Matthew 18:18).

Greater is He who is in me than the one who is in the world (1 John 4:4).

I don't have a spirit of fear but a spirit of power, a sound mind and self-control (2 Timothy 1:7).

The joy of the Lord is my strength (Psalm 28:7).

The Bible is a legal document, sealed by the blood of Jesus. It is our believing and confessing makes it a reality to us. Let us say what the Word of God says about us and our situation. To sum up: I have been delivered, healed, set free and made whole (Isaiah 53:5; Matthew 8:16-17).

Concluding Remarks

I am identified with Christ – He is my substitute and my representative;

I have died with Christ – His death was my death;

My failures and bondages were buried with Christ;

His victory was my victory – His triumph was my triumph;

I was raised with Christ – I shared in his glorious resurrection;

I am seated with Christ in heavenly places at the right hand of the Father – a place of authority;

God identified me with Christ – therefore I can't lose!

Chapter 17

THE LORD'S SUPPER

For this is My blood of the new covenant, which is shed
for many for the remission of sins. (Matthew 26:28 NKJV)

Introduction

Jesus gave His disciples the two ordinances, Baptism and the Lord's Supper, whereby they could show their allegiance to Him. In this chapter, we will focus on the Lord's Supper. The Lord's Supper (1 Corinthians 11:20), is a visible representation of the good news of the death of Christ for our sins. It reminds us of Christ's death and the glorious hope of His return. Our participation in it strengthens our faith through fellowship with Christ and with other believers. The term 'Breaking of Bread' (Acts 2:42) refers to the Lord's Supper also known as Holy Communion. We call it the Lord's Supper because it is His supper, not ours. When we have Communion, Jesus wants to come and have fellowship with us as we partake of the Lord's Supper. There is communion in the Communion (see 1 Corinthians 10:16).

What Does the Lord's Supper Mean?

The early church remembered that Jesus instituted the Lord's Supper on the night of the Passover meal (Luke 22:13-20). Just as Passover celebrated deliverance from slavery in Egypt, so the Lord's Supper celebrates deliverance from sin by Christ's death. Jesus Christ took bread and wine, and used them as a picture or symbol of His body and His blood. By breaking bread together and sharing the cup together, the disciples were doing what Jesus Christ had asked. He instituted and requested (Matthew 26:26-30; Mark 14:22-25; Luke 22:19-20) this before He died on the cross, in order that they might keep Him continually in their minds. Every believer should do the same, according to the Word of God. The disciples would not at that time have understood the full significance of what Jesus Christ had said and done, but He knew the painful truth. He had come to give His body and shed His life's blood for the sins of the world, and therefore took the simple elements of bread and wine to portray these profound truths.

Paul gives a careful account of the beginning of the Lord's Supper, and then tells of its value (1 Corinthians 11:23-33):

1. It was established in the night in which Christ was betrayed (v 23).

2. It is celebrated in remembrance of Jesus' undying love for His followers (vv 24-25). Jesus Christ requested His disciples to continue regularly the simple service He had begun, in remembrance of Himself. When He instituted this service, He said, 'do this in remembrance of me'. The words 'do this' are in the present continuous tense, which means 'keep on doing this until He comes again'. We do this, by thinking about what He did and why He did it.

3. It was a symbol of His body which was broken for them. "Is not the cup of thanksgiving for which we give thanks a participation in the blood of Christ? And is not the bread that we break a participation in the Body of Christ? Because there is one loaf, we, who are many, are one body, for we all partake of the one loaf", 1 Corinthians 10:16-17.

4. It was a new covenant in His blood (v 25). In the old covenant, people could approach God only through the priest and the sacrificial system. Jesus' death on the cross ushered in the new covenant or agreement between God and us. It is important for us to realise that now all people can personally approach God and communicate with Him. The new covenant completes, rather than replaces the old covenant, fulfilling anything the old covenant looked forward to (Jeremiah 31:31-34). Eating the bread and drinking the cup shows that we are remembering Christ's death for us and renewing our commitment to serve Him.

5. It was a pledge of His coming again. "For whenever you eat this bread and drink this cup you proclaim the Lord's death until he comes" (v 26).

Specific Instructions

Paul gives specific instructions how the Lord's Supper should be observed:

1. We should take the Lord's Supper thoughtfully because we are proclaiming that Christ died for our sins (v 26).

2. We should take it worthily, with due reverence and respect (v 27).

3. We should examine ourselves for any un-confessed sins or

resentful attitudes. We are to be properly prepared, based on our belief in and love for Christ (v 28).

4. We should discern the Lord's Body (v 29b) - some of the Corinthian church, had been using this time to selfishly feast, not considering the rest of the Body of Christ (brethren) and not for remembering what Jesus did.

5. We should be considerate of others, waiting until everyone is there and then eating in an orderly and unified manner (v 33).

When we take Communion, we must not rush into it without thinking of its meaning, "without recognising the body of the Lord" (v 29), and honouring His sacrifice. We can prepare ourselves for communion through healthy introspection leading to repentance and resolution of differences with others. The Lord's Supper is not to be taken lightly; this new covenant cost Jesus His life. It is not a meaningless ritual but an ordinance given by Christ to help strengthen our faith.

How Do We Feed on Jesus?

Spiritually, feeding on Jesus' body and drinking His blood will fill us with His very life. Food gives us nourishment, strength, and satisfaction. Jesus is our spiritual source of nourishment, strength and satisfaction. "Then Jesus declared, 'I am the bread of life'. He who comes to me will never go hungry, and he who believes in me will never be thirsty", John 6:35. We feed on Jesus by coming to Him and believing in Him. Coming to Him means having a heart that is drawn toward Jesus. We are to seek God with all of our heart, mind, and strength. We receive from God by faith.

Jesus taught His disciples to remember His sacrifice for them. "And he took bread, gave thanks and broke it, and gave to them, saying, 'This is my body given for you; do this in remembrance of me.' In the same way, after the supper he took the cup saying, 'this cup is the new covenant in my blood, which is poured out for you'", Luke 22:19-20. We are to partake of communion to remember His broken body and the blood that Jesus shed for us.

When we take Communion, we can say – 'we receive this bread as a symbol of Your flesh, Lord, and this wine as a symbol of Your precious blood. Lord, we are doing this in remembrance of You; we are proclaiming Your death on the cross until You come'. As partakers of the blood of Jesus we have the Holy Spirit empowering us to give our lives to God and serve Him in the Spirit of Holiness. It is important to God that we remember what He has done for us. That is why we celebrate the Lord's Supper – to remember all the good things He has done for us through the cross.

How Do We Remember Christ in the Lord's Supper?

We do this, by thinking about what He did and why He did it. If the Lord's Supper becomes just a ritual or a pious habit, it no longer remembers Christ, and it loses its significance. Christ wants us to remember Him! Think of Christ when we go to His Table. He longs for our love! Let us remind ourselves of the deep spiritual significance of this Supper. Like the disciples on the Emmaus Road (Luke 24:30), we break bread with our risen Lord, who comes in power to save us, heal us and bless us. Jesus said, "I tell you the truth, unless you can eat the flesh of the Son of Man and drink his blood, you have no life in you. Whoever eats my flesh and drinks my blood has eternal life, and I will raise him up at the last day", John 6:53-54.

Faith at the Lord's Table, Faith Confession

"Just as the act of water baptism outwardly declares or confesses an inward experience of salvation through the blood of the Lord Jesus, each observances of the Lord's Table is a powerful occasion for faith confession. In the ordinance, the Christian confesses before all heaven that he not only has believed, but that he has not forgotten. 'In remembrance' involves more than just memory; the word suggests an 'active calling to mind' (Wycliffe). The word 'for' introduces the reason the Supper is continually repeated. It is an acted sermon, for it 'proclaims' the Lord's death. The outward act of faith, as the bread and cup taken, is explicitly said to be an ongoing, active confession or proclaiming (1 Corinthians 11:26). Each occasion of partaking is an opportunity to say, proclaim, or confess again: 'I herewith lay hold of all the benefits of Jesus Christ's full redemption for my life – forgiveness, wholeness, strength, health, sufficiency'. The Lord's Supper is not to be simply a ritual remembrance, but an active confession, by which you actively will to call to memory and appropriate today all that Jesus has provided and promised through His cross"[1].

As we ponder over the benefits found in Psalm 103, we can declare in faith that, I am forgiven (v 3); I am healed (v 3); I am redeemed (v 4); I am crowned with love and compassion (v 4); I am satisfied with good things (v 5); I am renewed like the eagle (v 5). Our God is a good God. "I will make an everlasting covenant with them: I will never stop doing good to them....I will rejoice in doing them good...with all my heart and soul", Jeremiah 32:40-41.

Concluding Remarks

Holy Communion is a memorial of Jesus Christ's body being broken for sin and sickness, and His blood being shed to atone for sin. It is instituted by Jesus Himself, He asked disciples to do it in His memory. When we participate in its commemoration, we are testifying that Jesus Christ died for us and shed His blood for us. We are remembering what He did for us. Every time we partake of the elements in commemoration of the Lord's Supper, we are giving personal testimony that Jesus Christ rose from the dead and He is alive today.

During Communion, when both elements are given out, it is good if there is time before partaking of them to talk with God and examine ourselves and also a time for a prayer of thanksgiving for what He has done for us.

Let us conclude this study in the words of the song by Janet Lunt:

Refrain   "Broken for me, broken for you.
                      The body of Jesus broken for you.

He offered his body he poured out his soul,

Jesus was broken that we might be whole:

Come to my table and with me dine,

Eat of my bread and drink of my wine:

This is my body given for you,

Eat it remembering I died for you:

This is my blood I shed for you,

For your forgiveness, making you new:"[2]

Whenever we celebrate the Lord's Supper, we must remember that it is because of the blood of Jesus Christ that we can have fellowship with God and because He bore our sicknesses in His body that we can receive healing.

Chapter 18

THE MINISTRY OF THE CHURCH

. . .Christ is the head of the church, his body,
of which he is the Saviour. (Ephesians 5:23)

Introduction

The first New Testament mention of the church was by Jesus. ". . . on this rock I will build my church, and the gates of Hades will not overcome it", Matthew 16:18. It is God's intention that those He calls from everywhere into one body will grow in unity, knowledge, stature, strength, love, and skilfulness and become, a force that cannot be prevailed against. "But Saul began to destroy the church. Going from house to house, he dragged off men and women and put them in prison", Acts 8:3. Saul had been persecuting the church but Jesus took it personally! "As he neared Damascus on his journey, suddenly a light from heaven flashed around him. He fell to the ground and heard a voice say to him, 'Saul, Saul, why do you persecuting me?' 'Who are you, Lord?' Saul asked. 'I am Jesus, whom you are persecuting', he replied. 'Now get up and go into the city, and you will be told what you must do'", Acts 9:3-6. What Jesus seeks to do as head of the church, to form believers by uniting them in proper order to become one body, one holy temple, a church filled with His power to facilitate His will.

God called each of us believers 'out of and into'; we were called out off old, godless and self-centred lives into new, alive, God-glorifying and God-centred lives. The root meaning of church (*ecclesia* in Greek) is 'called-out ones', the body of believers gather to worship Jesus. Every believer is what makes up the church, the Body of Christ. Every born-again believer is in Jesus, who is head of the church. We are members of the church that belongs to Jesus. Therefore, we need to find a group of Christians that meet together on a regular basis, under the leadership of a minister or a pastor (local church), where we receive solid Biblical doctrine, experience healthy, loving and confronting relationships whereby we can be challenged to grow up spiritually and fulfil God's plan for our lives.

The Birth of the Church

On the day of Pentecost, through the descent and baptism in the Holy Spirit, all living believers were incorporated into the church, the Body of Christ, through which the absent Lord Jesus continues His work in the world (see Acts 2:1-47). That day was marked by miraculous signs (vv 1-13), an explanatory sermon by Peter (vv 14-40), and salvation of some three thousand people (vv 41-47).

What Jesus Christ Is to the Church

1. He is the head of the body, that is, of the church. The church is the Body of Christ (Colossians 1:18), that is, the organism through which He acts and which shares all His experiences. Jesus Christ is the guiding Spirit of the church; it is at His bidding that the

church must live and move. "For in him we live and move and have our being", Acts 17:28. Without Jesus, the church cannot think the truth, cannot act correctly, cannot decide its direction because the body is the servant of the head and is powerless without it.

2. He is the beginning of the church. The world is the creation of Christ. "...all things were created by him and for him", Colossians 1:16b; and church is the new creation of Christ. Christ is the source of the church's life and being and the director of its continued activity. He is the Lord of all, by virtue of His victory over death. By His resurrection, He has shown that He has conquered every opposing power and that there is nothing in life or in death which can bind Him. That is the authority He has delegated to the church (Matthew 28:18-20).

The Three Important Ministries of the Church

1. A ministry to God

Worshipping God is one of the important ministries of the church. We not only minister to God in worship as individual believers but also minister to God in corporate worship as the church. When the church worships God, it is not just to fill time or prepare hearts for the Word. We worship with all our heart, lift up our hands to God, and offer up the spiritual sacrifice, the fruit of our lips giving thanks (Hebrews 13:15) and touching our spirit with His Spirit, the passionate worship of our heart. Our words of worship are our offering.

Worship is far more than a 'song service'. It is our priestly calling. This significant ministry of the church is a ministry unto God. We lift our hearts, our hands, our voices, and our sacrifices of praise unto God. "...let us continually offer to God a sacrifice of praise

– the fruit of lips that confess his name", Hebrews 13:15. Praise is our homage to God who is incomparably great. The final psalm (150) is a summons to everyone. It invites us all to worship: 'Let everything that has breath praise the Lord' (v 6), 'for His surpassing greatness' (v 2). Singing is an important part of the Christian life, for it enables us to praise God. We should praise the Lord because of His redemption, the revelation of His righteousness, and the remembrance of His mercy, love and faithfulness (Psalm 98:1-3).

Our praise should come from the Holy Spirit within (Ephesians 5:18-20) and be based on Scripture (Colossians 3:16). In this way, we worship Him 'in spirit and in truth' (John 4:24). We worship Him because of who God is and what God does. The better we know God, the more we will worship Him. The more we experience His grace in daily life, the more praise we will bring to Him. We worship Him because:

We are a nation of priests – " But you are a chosen people, a royal priesthood, a holy nation, a people belonging to God, that you may declare the praises of him who called you out of darkness into His wonderful light", 1 Peter 2:9. We are set apart people; we have a 'high calling'; we have a purpose for living. Therefore our spiritual sacrifices are the passionate words of love, worship, appreciation and thanks that burn on the altar of our hearts.

We are chosen by God – "For he chose us in him before the creation of the world to be holy and blameless in his sight", Ephesians 1:7. "Therefore, as God's chosen people, holy and dearly beloved, clothe yourselves with compassion, kindness, humility, gentleness and patience. Bear with each other and forgive whatever grievances you may have against one another. Forgive as the Lord forgave you. Over all these virtues put on love, which binds them altogether in perfect unity", Colossians 3:1-4.

We are royal priesthood and a holy nation – 1) We are to reflect the holiness of God in our daily living. "But just as he who called is holy, so be holy in all you do; for it is written: 'Be holy, because I am holy'", 1 Peter 1:15-16. 2) Sacrifice – "Therefore, I urge you, brothers, in view of God's mercy to offer your bodies as living sacrifices, holy and pleasing to God – this is your spiritual act of worship", Romans 12:1. 3) Intercession – "...he offered up prayers and petitions..." Hebrews 5-7. "I urge you then, first of all, that requests, prayers, intercession and thanksgiving be made for everyone", 1 Timothy 2:1. 4) Reflecting God's character and nature, – "We are therefore Christ's ambassadors, as though God were making his appeal through us", 2 Corinthians 5:20.

We are people belonging to God – God's own possession. "who gave himself for us to redeem us from all wickedness and to purify for himself a people that are his very own, eager to do what is good", Titus 2:14.

2. Ministry of edification and caring for one another

In this ministry, we open our hearts to each other and the needs of the church body, we reach in to give, and we open our mouths to teach, encourage and challenge one another. Yes, we open our hearts, open our mouths and open our hands one to another. Interestingly, the New Testament says a significant amount about believers caring for one another. "But God has combined the members of the body and has given greater honour to the parts that lacked it, so that there should be no division in the body, but that its parts should have equal concern for each other", 1 Corinthians 12:24-25. God's will is that believers care for one another. The hearts contributes, the eyes contributes, the ears contributes, the feet contributes; every member supplies something. When the body is healthy, the body works and produces. Beloved, let us love one another. When we care for one another we become strong and healthy. From this place of strength and health, we can work concentrating on the harvest and the lost.

"When he had finished washing...", John 13:12-15. In this profound example, Jesus gave His disciples a clear message: "You ought to care for one another". This is one of the ministries of the church. "A new command I give you: Love one another...", John 13:34-35. Just as Jesus charged His disciples: "Go and make disciples of all nations" (Matthew 28:18-20), He also charged them: "Love one another".

One of the hallmarks of the church is encouraging one another and spur one another on towards love, good deeds and service. That is where the Body of Christ, the church comes in by providing:

A place to belong – A church is a place where followers of Jesus come together by His Spirit. A local church is a place where you can go and join this family, it is a place to belong. A church is where we meet with other believers for worship, teaching, encouragement, and service (see Hebrews 10:25; Romans 12:5).

A place to serve – Christians need to be involved in a local church so that they can discover their function and use their gifts. In a world of self-centred people, Christ's example and command to serve others still applies (see Romans 12:6; 1 Corinthians 14:26).

A place to be served – As Christians serve within the church, they will find God meeting many of their own needs through others. Church members need to depend on each other just as the parts of the body do (see John 13:34; 1 Corinthians 12:14-27).

A place to grow – Just as our physical bodies need nourishment to develop and grow to maturity, so too our spiritual lives need to be fed. This spiritual food includes worship, instruction, and counsel. We need to be taught and challenged by gifted and experienced teachers who know God's Word. And often we need to be encouraged by those who really care about us.

A place to obey – The Christian faith is personal: "By this all men will know that you are my disciples, if you love one another", John 13:35. Jesus said, "If you hold to my teaching you are my disciples", John 8:31[1].

3. The ministry of evangelism

The one main functions of the church, as it relates to the world is evangelism as commissioned by our Lord Himself. In our ministry to the world we open our hearts to the lost. We stretch out our arms, embracing the broken and laying hands on the sick. We open our mouths and declare the glorious Gospel of Jesus Christ. Before leaving the earth, in the Great Commission, Jesus told His disciples, "All authority in heaven...to the very end of the age", Matthew 28:18-20. Five things Jesus emphasised in the Great Commission given: 1) Go; 2) Make disciples; 3) Baptise them; 4) Teach them to obey; 5) I will be with you always. Jesus' saving mission, the full measure of His gifting, and authority to speak and work in His Name was transferred to the Body of Christ, the church. Paul's words to the Philippians describe who the church is and our ministry to the lost. "so that you may become blameless and pure, children of God without fault in a crooked and depraved generation, in which you shine like stars in the universe as you hold out the word of life", 2:15-16a.

We are children of God. We shine as lights in the world. And we hold forth the Word of Life to those who are lost. "But you will receive power when the Holy Spirit comes on you; and you will be my witnesses in Jerusalem, and in all Judea and Samaria, and to the ends of the earth", Acts 1:8. God always looks for a man on earth to work with Him to do His will. God is also looking for a body through which He can speak, work and express. The body He has chosen in this dispensation is the Body of Christ, the church. Let the world hear His call, experience His love, and be touched by His power. Church is a lamp. Without passion, sound doctrine, strong leadership and pastoral care, the lamp would diminish in brightness and fail in the purpose for which they were lit and placed by God.

The Characteristics of a Healthy Church

We read in Acts 9:31 that "then the church throughout Judea, Galilee and Samaria enjoyed a time of peace. It was strengthened; and encouraged by the Holy Spirit, it grew in numbers, living in the fear of the Lord". Those early local churches (Acts 9:23-43) were characterised by:

Peace (v 31) – because they had learned to rest in the living God, despite of all forms of persecution.

Edification (v 31) – for sound teaching is a vital feature of any church that would honour the truth. Spiritual preaching produces conviction, and genuine conversion, which is marked by continuance in the things of God (see Acts 2:37, 41-47). Paul wrote to Timothy, "Until I come, devote yourself to the public reading of the Scripture, to preaching and to teaching", 1 Timothy 4:13.

They were known for reverence, walking in the 'fear of the Lord' – We need a deeper appreciation of our God's greatness, vastness and uniqueness.

They experienced the counsel of the Holy Spirit – to direct the saints in worship and testimony to the Lord Jesus.

As a result, they were multiplied – A shallow Christianity in the assembly may draw crowds but it cannot change lives.

Where Do We Fit into the Church

No matter what we are required to do by God, first and foremost we are a member of the church or a 'sheep' that belong to Jesus who is called 'the Chief Shepherd' (see 1 Peter 5:4). God has appointed some people roles of leadership within the church to help the members of the church to grow spiritually, these are commonly known as 'spiritual leaders' and this includes role of the pastor in our lives (see Ephesians 4:7-16). A big part of the pastor's role is to 'feed the sheep' or in other words to teach the people what the Bible says and how to live by that. They also have the role of protecting the church from false teaching. We should keep a good attitude towards spiritual leaders, following them as we see how they live, honouring them and praying for them. However, we all have a role to play as a part of the church and our job with the guidance of the Holy Spirit and our spiritual leaders is to find what that is and to function in it. Every part of the Body of Christ is valuable and necessary (see 1 Corinthians 12).

Concluding Remarks

A nation of priests to worship God; members of one body to care for one another; the light of the world to show God to the lost. This is who the church is and what the church does. The Body of Christ is designed by God to edify itself in love. Love is also meeting the needs of one another. It is a command. According to Ephesians 4:12, the saints need to be edified (built up) for two goals: 'for the equipping of the saints for the work of service' and enable them to grow in spiritual maturity. They also need to be equipped to perform that role (work) in the Body of Christ that God wants them to perform. The ultimate ministry of the church is to bring glory and honour to its head, Jesus Christ.

The commission of the Risen Jesus is to go out and to make the kingdom of the world into the kingdom of God (Matthew 28:19). The task of the Christian is to be by word and by life the witness of Jesus (Acts 1:8). We are to preach a message of repentance and the remission of sins (Luke 24:47). Jesus given us an explanation of the meaning of history and the culmination of history in Himself (Luke 24:27; 44-46). With the commission and the task He gave us the power to carry them out (Acts 1:8), and a promise to be with us (Matthew 28:20). The Bible says, "The fruit of the righteous is a tree of life, and he who wins souls is wise", Proverbs 11:30. "Those who are wise will shine like the brightness of the heavens, and those who lead many to righteousness, like the stars forever and ever", Daniel 12:3.

Finally, love one another is a recurrent New Testament theme. We can show love in many ways: By avoiding prejudice and discrimination, by accepting people, by listening, helping, giving, serving, and refusing to judge. A church with an atmosphere of love, forgiveness and acceptance is the type of church in which we will grow and blossom – where we need sound doctrine, we need fellowship, we need the breaking of bread and we need prayer and worship.

Chapter 19

MARRIAGE AND FAMILY LIFE

The LORD God said, "It is not good for the man to be alone.
I will make a helper suitable for him." (Genesis 2:18)

Introduction

God established marriage to meet man's need for companionship (Genesis 2:18) and to provide for the rearing of children (Genesis 1:28). 'Marriage is the building block of human society and is at the centre of God's purposes', says G. & M. Norridge. The Lord told Adam and Eve to "be fruitful and increase in number; fill the earth and subdue it. Rule...." (Genesis 1:28) or as Eugene Peterson puts it in The Message, "Prosper! Reproduce! Fill the earth! Take charge! Be responsible....for every living thing that moves on the face of the earth". The Bible begins with a marriage – Adam and Eve (Genesis 2:23-25) – and ends with a marriage – Christ and the Church (Revelation 21:2). Throughout the Bible, marriage is often used as a prophetic picture of God's relationship with His people"[1].

The growth, maturity and happiness of one's marriage is not just determined by God but by one's desire and capacity for personal knowledge. The only thing that can stop one's marriage from success is lack of knowledge and corresponding action. Nobody has success without having the attitude of a conqueror. We must have the attitude of a conqueror and triumph in marriage in Christ Jesus. If we can't rejoice in the differences between men and women, we will never experience the marriage relationship as divinely intended. Our spouses can be so different to us, but we can share those complementary strengths with each other and help make up for the other's weaknesses.

Marriage

Marriage is God's idea (Genesis 2:18-24). Creation was incomplete without both sexes (male and female). "So God created man in his own image, in the image of God he created him; male and female he created them", Genesis 1:27. God's plan for them was to be together. At the very beginning God instituted marriage (Genesis 2:24). Marriage was designed by God to resolve the first human problem of solitude. Hence, it was created to give happiness. The goal in marriage should be more than just friendship, it should be oneness. The oneness between the Father and the Son is an example for us. "I and the Father are one", John 10:30. God gave marriage as a gift to Adam and Eve. They were created perfect for each other. Marriage was not just for convenience, nor was it brought about by any culture. It was instituted by God and has three basic aspects. "For this reason a man will leave his father and mother and be united to his wife, they will become one flesh", Genesis 2:24:

- The man leaves his parents and in a public act, promises himself to his wife.

- The man and woman are joined together (cleaving) by taking responsibility for each other's welfare and by loving their mate above all others.

- The two become one flesh in the intimacy and commitment of sexual union that is reserved for marriage. Strong marriages include all three of these aspects.

Some important truths about marriage:

Marriage is a gift from God – God instituted marriage. It is a covenant (mutual agreement) between a man and a woman with God. There must be the fear of God and total commitment in married life.

Marriage is a calling – We are called to marry each other to love, to submit and be considerate, respectful and offer mutual support.

Marriage is a ministry – As we grow in the Lord and in marriage we should minister to God, each other and to others. Building a Christian home is a great ministry. Marriage should create the best environment for raising children.

Marriage is a blessing from God – Marriage is a living symbol of Christ and the church; good and honourable; principled practise of love; a firm commitment of faithfulness, honesty, respect, affection, attention and encouragement and a bond of trust.

Marriage is a challenge – The burdens that marriage brings can be difficult at times. We have to learn to understand each other's weakness and strength and be kind and tender-hearted to each other in mutual submission and affection. Be over-comers and conquerors; Love each other and function as one, letting God be at the centre.

Commitment is essential to successful marriage – Marriage creates the best environment for raising children "Because he was seeking godly offspring", Malachi 2:15.

Marriage is permanent. Ideally, only death should dissolve marriage (Matthew 19:6). Marriage is based on the principled practise of love, not on feelings (Ephesians 5:21-33).

Marriage is an investment – for profit and great return for which thoughtful planning and execution is required daily, based on the Word of God.

Marriage is not just sharing the same bed, but having the same values and the same goals in order to reach the same destination and follow the same road map. T. D. Jake says, "When we know we are loved because of who we are, we become healthier in mind and more intimate in expression. Because we are free from the fear of rejection and loosed from the anxiety of having to perform".

Failure of Responsibility

When the devil came as a serpent and put doubt into Eve's mind, Adam failed to exercise his authority over the serpent. Instead of taking responsibility for himself he chose to blame his wife.

Eliminate the common errors made by Adam (Genesis 1:26):

- Adam failed to understand his God-given responsibility and authority.

- Adam failed to recognise resistant forces in completing the plan of God. God gave Adam a beautiful help-mate but he failed to protect her.

- Adam failed to recognise the true God-quality of love to help lead his marriage. Love always looks to give at the expense of self, which in turn produces a harvest of blessing.

Family Life

The family began: "Male and female he created them", Genesis 1:27. The building of a godly home is most important. The Bible lays down the principles. Marriage is a lifetime commitment (1 Corinthians 7:39a). There is to be no unequal yoke (2 Corinthians 6:14). It is based on mutual love and respect (Ephesians 5:22-25). Children born into such a home are the fruit and joy of parents (Psalm 127:3-5). The Bible has much to say about the husband in a home. He is the head and God will hold him responsible for leadership and kindly discipline in the home. If husband is the head then his wife is the heart. She is like a fruitful vine, and the children like olive plants around the table (Psalm 128:3). The godly home is God's masterpiece, and is a most attractive and pleasant place built upon the foundation of the Word. The greatest joy is to see one's children walk in truth (3 John v 4; Psalm 128:6). The Christian family should portray Christ in this present world. A family who is walking in covenant relationship with God will be a visible picture of Christ and the church.

Heavenly Home on Earth

Every member of a Christian home must be able to take responsibility for themselves. Home must be a place where every member can come and have fellowship, recharge and reorganise as necessary and go out again into the world. There are different kinds of influence outside the home such as friends, media, school, church etc. Parents have a responsibility to let children know that their significance does not resting on what the world sees as performance, but their position in Christ Jesus (Ephesians 1:5-9). It is important to God that every generation understands his ways. It is parent's responsibility to keep a check on bitterness or strife among children (James 4:1-3). At the same time to respect the privacy of each individual. It is advisable to get to know our children's friends, their behaviour and interests. Bad company corrupts good character (1 Corinthians 15:33-34).

Church Family

We are called to be involved in the local church for worship, teaching, encouragement and service. We are given by God's Spirit, special spiritual gifts and important tasks as well as ordinary things to do. The family needs to be involved in serving in the Body of Christ, the local church. As we serve within the church, we will find God meeting many of our own needs through others. We are also taught and challenged by gifted, ordained and experienced ministers of God, pastors/teachers who know God's Word. For the spiritual growth of the family we need to plant ourselves in a local church. It is a place to practise both a new and growing faith and a mature and wise faith. Hence, our involvement and commitment in the local church as a family is a priority and not optional. It is a command of our Lord. Marriage is teamwork as is the work in the church, everybody working together in for the mission of Christ.

Being Single

Six things about being single:

1. It is an opportunity and not a problem, so one does not have to strive or try to make the things happen, worried that you are running out of time.

2. It is an opportunity to stretch our faith in God and find out God's will.

3. It is an opportunity to get to know God and oneself. God will supply all our needs.

4. It is an opportunity to learn to reign alone.

5. It is a good chance to prepare ourselves to add value to the person we will marry.

6. It is a chance to analyse one's dreams and goals and get a plan for success in God.

As a single person, don't just settle for any mate. Go to God and tell Him what you would like, being open to His input and get a plan for successful future which will remain with you even after marriage. Be realistic and follow the guidance of the Holy Spirit.

When you know in your heart that you have met the right person God has for you to marry, act in faith avoiding doubts and fears and be expectant that God will help you both. It is important to have divine assurance and peace regarding our decision of who to marry. Involve and seek counsel from your spiritual leader in the process.

Concluding Remarks

God created marriage, encourages it and commands unity in it as a lifelong relationship. It was the first institution. Responsibility for marriage is on the man's shoulder – he is to 'leave' his father and his mother, thus establishing his own authority or autonomy in marriage. The responsibility for keeping the union together is on man's shoulder – he is to 'cleave' to his wife in total loyalty and act of love in marriage. The union is indissoluble – they shall become 'one flesh' assuming new identity. Both husband and wife must make a deliberate effort to deposit into the marriage in order to draw out of it. It was God's original plan for a man to marry a woman and have intimate relationship with each other. If we can't appreciate and rejoice in the difference between being man and woman we will never obtain divine relationship as God has ordained marriage. Praying together in the home is a vital key for staying together. Every father is responsible before God to maintain day-to-day intercession for his whole household.

Parents must take responsibility to maintain a standard and daily protection for children and have good communication with each other. Administering godly order in the home in love brings peace. Marriage was created to bring happiness, fellowship and fulfilment. We have the Holy Spirit in us and by the help of Him we can avoid pitfalls by walking in love, which is the most powerful force. We can choose to walk together and win the trophy, everybody knowing their position in the family and functioning harmoniously (1 Peter 1:13-16).

In marriage we must learn 'to submit one another out of reverence for Christ' (Ephesians 5:21); encourage one another (1 Thessalonians 5:11); forgiving one another (Ephesians 4:32); pray for each other; spur one another on toward love and good deed (Hebrews 10:24); carry each other's burdens; and giving preference to one another (Romans 12:10).

Chapter 20

THE GIFTS AND THE FRUIT OF THE HOLY SPIRIT

Now to each one the manifestation of the Spirit
is given for the common good. (1 Corinthians 12:7)

A. The Gifts of the Holy Spirit

Introduction

First Corinthians chapter twelve was written for correction and instruction to the Corinthian believers who were operating in the gifts already. Apostle Paul did not want them to be ignorant of the gifts as it causes believers to withdraw from the gifts. God cannot bless ignorance. The Holy Spirit is the giver of spiritual gifts (vv 1-11). Gifts of the Spirit are harvesting tools for saving people. These gifts are divine equipments and divine assistance. We need to recognise that 'who we are in Christ' for the manifestation of the Holy Spirit to operate in our lives. And how to get the power of the Holy Spirit through us for being a blessing by doing good to others. John 15:7, "If you remain in me and my words remain in you, ask whatever you wish and it will be given you", is a platform for the gift of the Holy Spirit. It will help us to activate power to do the will of our Father in heaven, as Jesus did.

The gifts of the Spirit are the rivers of living water that Jesus talked about in John 7:38 NKJV. "He who believes in Me, as the Scripture has said, out of his heart will flow rivers of living water". It emphasises the plurality of 'rivers' in relation to the different types of gifts. A spiritual gift may be defined as any ability that is empowered by the Holy Spirit and used in many ministry of the church. Spiritual gifts are given to equip the church to carry out its ministry until Christ's return. Paul reminds believers in the use of spiritual gifts, they are to 'try to excel in gifts that build up the church' (1 Corinthians 14:12). Spiritual gifts are apportioned to each person individually by the Holy Spirit 'just as he determines' (1 Corinthians 12:11). John 14:6 is the platform for the demonstration of the Holy Spirit - "I am the way and the truth and the life". The key to operate in the Spirit is found in verse 10 of the same chapter – "Don't you believe that I am in the Father, and that the Father is in me? The words I say to you are not just my own. Rather, it is the Father, living in me, who is doing his work". The door way to the gifts of the Spirit is to demand in Jesus' name – "You may ask me for anything in my name, and I will do it", John 14:14. There are nine spiritual gifts. All these gifts are supernatural.

Diversities of Spiritual Gifts

There are diversities of gifts (1 Corinthians 12:1-11), but all these groups flow from only one source: The Holy Spirit of God. Some of the gifts are plural, for example, gifts of healings, working of miracles, discerning of spirits, kinds of tongues. We must remember that all these are gifts of God's grace. They are received by faith. We can never earn them. Within the nine gifts of the Spirit there are three groups:

Power gifts

God imparts His own divine powers and abilities to man. It includes:

Special faith – It is a mantle of faith that comes on us for someone else. This manifestation is a spirit of knowing for divine assistance for a brief moment at a time. It is a carrier of miracles. Obedience is the doorway for special faith. The platform for special faith is having a revelation of authority in the name of Jesus. Boldness is required to operate in this gift. We must act in obedience with boldness when special faith comes on us. Example of this is 'the lame man was healed' as found in Acts chapter 3:5-6,16 (see also Acts 9:33-35). The gift of special faith was in operation on Apostle Peter. In special faith we believe in such a way that God honours our word when we speak without doubt.

Working of miracles – It is a person doing a supernatural act by the divine power of the Holy Spirit. Miracles are a bi-product of authority given by our Lord Jesus. A supernatural occurrence is called a miracle because it is beyond our natural comprehension. Working of miracles is active through a human instrument. Obedience is the doorway for the miracles. An example of this is found in Acts chapter 5:1-14. After Ananias and Sapphira dropped dead, "Great fear seized the whole church and all who heard about these events" (v 11). We can also see an example of working of miracle at the 'wedding of Cana' (John 2:1-11). 'Working of miracles' is active, doing something in obedience to His Word. It operates closely with the gifts of faith and healings to bring authority over sin, Satan, sickness and the binding of forces of this age.

Gifts of healings – In the gifts of healings, God supernaturally heals the sick through a ministry anointed by the Holy Spirit. Number one way to operate in the gifts of healings is to magnify God for His power, His mercy, His goodness and the finished work of the cross of Jesus. Magnifying God builds a platform for gifts of healings to manifest. On the other hand, tradition and unbelief can stand in the way. In Acts chapter 8, we see Philip was operating in the gifts of healings, and healings and miracles happened. As a result, many people got saved and they were filled with joy.

Revelation gifts

The infinite God is revealing His truth to man. The revelation gifts is a doorway to the power gifts. It includes:

Word of knowledge – is a supernatural revelation of the divine will and plan by the Holy Spirit concerning people, places or things. It is a revelation of a fact that exists and it will be a doorway to the miracles. It is divine assistance relating to the present or past and usually comes in a fragment of a word or a sentence. For example, Jesus telling Nathanael about how He saw him under the fig tree and that in him there was no deceit (John 1:47-48); In Acts 10, Apostle Peter receives a word of knowledge in a vision.

Words of wisdom – is the revealing of the prophetic future under the anointing of God. In this, knowledge is rightly applied: wisdom works interactively with knowledge and discernment. Sometimes it can be a warning! For example, the revelation that the Lord gave to Ananias, that He had called Paul to preach to the Gentiles (Acts 9:15).

Discerning spirits – is a gift of the Holy Spirit by which the possessor is enabled to see supernaturally into spirit world. It includes seeing Jesus, angels of God or demon spirit. In this gift we will see 'something', not a sense or perception. Purpose of it is to accelerate the plan or the will of God. Example of this is found in Acts 12:11.

Vocal gifts

Prophecy – It is a supernatural proclamation or an inspired utterance in known tongue, to amplify what God has already said in His Word. The inspired utterance is given for edification, exhortation and comfort to others. An example is found in Luke chapter 1:67-79. The spirit of prophecy is subject to the prophet (1 Corinthians 14:32).

Diverse kinds of tongues – They are a supernatural utterance by the Holy Spirit in a language never learned or understood by the speaker. It is beyond the intellect or lingualistic ability of man. Like prophecy, tongues and interpretation of tongues are vehicles for edification, exhortation and comfort to others. It serves as an evidence and sign of the indwelling and working of the Holy Spirit, for example, baptism in the Holy Spirit.

Interpretation of tongues – When a message in tongues has been given, then the interpretation of tongues goes into operation by supernatural power to reveal the meaning of tongues.

To sum up, we don't own any of these gifts. Magnifying the name of Jesus sets a platform for the gifts to operate and His name is the source of power in order to get people's attention drawn to Him. We must expect the Holy Spirit to flow through us and rejoice when people are blessed by the manifestation of the gifts of the Holy Spirit. God's wonderful mercy and love for people and also that God use these as a doorway for miracles and salvation. The gifts come within the whole context of the finished work of the cross; they point to the fact that Jesus was resurrected and He is alive and

God's general plan and purpose for mankind and of salvation. The key to operate in the Holy Spirit is love (1 Corinthians 12:31). The Spirit glorifies Christ (John 16:14), not Himself. The Spirit gives us gifts so that we can serve Christ and His church 'for the profit of all' (1 Corinthians 12:7). While nine fruits of the Spirit are given for character building, the gifts are given for demonstration of power as a harvesting tool to assist in harvest of souls. Now let us look at the opposite side of the coin:

B. Fruit of the Holy Spirit

What kind of person do we want to become? It is great to be known as a loving, joyful, peaceful, patient, kind, good, faithful, gentle, and self-controlled person. God has given us the Holy Spirit as He wants to transform us into that kind of person. In order to happen this, we must give God complete control of our life and allow the Holy Spirit to work in us. The Bible says "But the fruit of the Spirit is love, joy, peace, patience (long-suffering), kindness, goodness, faithfulness, gentleness and self-control" (Galatians 5:22-23a). The word 'Spirit' is with a capital 'S' – which means these nine fruits are coming directly from the Holy Spirit – not from us. Let us meditate on these specific nine qualities and uphold the importance of these nine specific fruits.

Nine Fruits of the Holy Spirit

The nine fruits of the Spirit can be divided into three groups. The first three (Love, Joy and Peace) concern our attitude toward God, the second triad (patience, kindness and goodness) deals with social relationships, and the third group (faithfulness, gentleness and self-control) describes principles that guide a Christian conduct. When the Spirit fully controls the life of a believer, he produces all of these graces.

First fruit of the Spirit is 'Love', is the primary form of fruit which manifests itself in rest of them. Derek Prince says, "Joy is love rejoicing; Peace is love resting; Long-suffering is love forbearing; Kindness is love serving others; Goodness is love seeking the best for others; Faithfulness is love keeping its promises; gentleness is love ministering to the hurts of others; Self-control is love in control"[1]. Jesus said in Matthew 7:20, NASB that "You will know them by their fruits".

Love – "is the ultimate expression of God's loyalty, purity, and mercy extended toward his people – to be reflected in human relationships of brotherly concern, marital fidelity, and adoration of God."[2] Hence, the extreme importance that God the Father is placing on that everyone learn how to love Him, love ourselves, love one another, and to even go as far as to be able to love our enemies and those who will try and hurt us (see 1 Thessalonians 4:9-10).

Joy – It is characterised by gladness and inner rejoicing in the Lord. The Bible says the joy of the Lord is our strength. Without God's joy operating in our lives, things can begin to dry up. The Holy Spirit will give us this joy when we yield to Him (see John 15:11).

Peace – Peace is a sense of well-being and fulfilment that comes from God and is dependent on His presence as well as harmony in personal relationship, especially with God. I have personally found that once we are in the Spirit, His peace starts to flow up into our mind, soul and inner being, as the Bible says 'a peace that surpasses all human understanding' (see John 14:27).

Patience (Long-suffering) – Patient endurance and steadfastness is exercised under provocation. One of the ways of our God is that He is a very patient and long-suffering God. His ways are not our ways. And one of the things we will find out very early on in our walk with Him about His ways that He works on a much slower time frame than we do. We all need the patience of the Holy Spirit to start operating in our souls and inner being (see Colossians 1:11).

Kindness – Kindness is the steadfast love that maintains relationships through grace and in times of need. The quality of kindness will go hand in hand with the quality of love (see Colossians 2:6).

Goodness – Goodness is beneficence (the quality of being kind), and ready to do good, love in action. The Bible says that it is the goodness of God that will lead sinners to repentance and salvation. If so, then the goodness of God operating through an anointed believer will have the ability to draw non-believers into salvation (see Psalm 25:8).

Faithfulness – Faithfulness is steadfast, dedicated, dependable and worthy of trust. Just as God will stay faithful to us in His own personal relationship to us He will expect us to stay loyal and faithful in our own personal relationships with God and others (see Matthew 25:21).

Gentleness – Gentleness is mildness combined with tenderness; a character that is equitable, reasonable, forbearing, moderate, fair and considerate. The quality of gentleness is another major quality needed in our lives and in our world today. Jesus is the perfect role model for all of us to study and learn from His earthly ministry (see Colossians 3:12).

Self-control – Self-control is sober, temperate, calm and dispassionate approach to life. The Bible tells us that our spirit and our flesh will war against each other in this life. And the only thing that will be able to curb and control some of the desires of our flesh is the quality of self-control. The Bible also tells us that if we learn how to really walk in the Holy Spirit then we will not fulfil the lust of our flesh (see Proverbs 25:28).

Concluding Remarks

The way to use the gifts that the Spirit gives is beautifully told in 1 Corinthians chapter 13. Love is the key that unlocks the door to all God has for us today. We are told that without 'love' these gifts add up to nothing. Love is the greatest way for gifts to happen and for ministry to mature. Manifestation of the Holy Spirit should not take centre stage – Jesus is our centre of focus. So, Christ will be exalted and others will be blessed.

The fruit of the Spirit are all very powerful in that they not only have ability to help change, transform and sanctify us but they also have the ability to touch all of those around us. Once the love of God starts to operate and flow through us to touch others, many or all of other eight fruits of the Holy Spirit will start to follow suite in domino fashion. Jesus is without question the ultimate role model, for all of us and of someone who was fully operating in all nine fruits of the Holy Spirit. These nine fruits will give us credibility with God and with other people that no degree or title can give us in this life.

Chapter 21

DIVINE HEALING

I am the LORD, who heals you.
(Exodus 15:26)

Introduction

Many believe that God is able to heal but they are not sure that He will heal them. It is God's will and desire for us to be healed, walking with Him in perfect health. Jesus went throughout Galilee ...healing every sickness and disease among the people (Matthew 4:23). Let us be open to the Word of God, "Heal me, O Lord, and I shall be healed", Jeremiah 17:14. The first covenant God set up for His new people Israel, after they had crossed the Red Sea, was the covenant of healing. This was distinctively a redemptive covenant – a privilege purchased by the blood of Christ through the atonement. Isaiah 53:4 tells us "surely he took up our infirmities and carried our sorrows". Throughout the Bible we read of the healing power of God and we believe what we read. Jesus is the same yesterday, today and forever. What God did in the Old Testament, and what Jesus did in the New Testament, He does today. Ministering healing is a wonderful opportunity to show God's love and compassion to people. Jesus has commissioned us to heal the sick. The authority that Jesus was given is the authority He now gives to us! This authority is mission focussed. Jesus has given us go ahead signal – 'Go and heal the sick' (see Matthew 10:1; Luke 10:9; Matthew 28:18-20; Mark 16:15-18).

Divine Healing Explained

The reasons for expecting and receiving healing from God:

God's very name is Healer

In the New Testament (under the new covenant), God reveals Himself fully through His Son, the Lord Jesus Christ. In the Old Testament we have some mighty and majestic revelations of the nature of God. The Lord is our Shepherd from that shepherd's Psalm, Psalm 23. In verse one we see God declaring himself to be Jehovah Roi – The Lord our Shepherd. Some other names by which God has revealed Himself to His people are:

God is Jehovah Rapha, I am the LORD who heals you (Exodus 15:26). God is our healer.

Jehovah Nissi, the LORD is my banner (Exodus 17:15). God is our banner.

Jehovah Jireh, the LORD will Provide (Genesis 22:14). God is our provider.

Jehovah Makadesh, I the LORD am Holy – I who make you holy (Leviticus 21:8). God is our sanctifier.

Jehovah Shalom, the LORD is Peace (Judges 6:24). God is our peace.

Jehovah Tsidkenu, the LORD our Righteousness (Jeremiah 23:5,6).

Jehovah Shamma, the LORD is there (Ezekiel 48:35). The God who is everpresent.

Yes, God is our everpresent One, He is our Provider, our Banner of Victory, our Peace, He is our Righteousness and our Shepherd and He is the One who sanctifies us. He is also the One who heals us. Let us learn to partake all of His attributes as revealed in His holy name. Divine healing clearly is ours, because our God has told us that He is Jehovah Rapha – I am the LORD who heals you. Psalm 103 verse 3 says, "who forgives all your sins and heals all your diseases".

Jesus was manifested to destroy the works of the devil

We know that sickness is an oppression and a bondage, the work of the evil one. The Bible says Jesus came to destroy the works of the devil. We read in 1 John 3:8 "...For this purpose the Son of God was manifested, that He might destroy the works of the devil" (NKJV). During His life on this earth He systematically overcame every enemy of man and finally even death, the last enemy of man. Jesus declared in Luke 4:18, "The Spirit of the Lord is upon Me, Because He has anointed Me to preach the gospel to the poor; He has sent Me to heal the broken-hearted, to proclaim liberty to the captives and recovery of sight to the blind, To set at liberty to those who are oppressed" (NKJV). He did that exactly and literally. "How God anointed Jesus of Nazareth with the Holy Spirit and power, and how he went around doing good and healing all who were under the power of the devil, because God was with him", Acts 10:38.

Healing is the children's bread

We read in Matthew 15:21-28, that Jesus heals the daughter of a Canaanite woman. Jesus tells her that healing is the children's bread. When we are God's children, healing is our portion at our Father's table because we are under the new covenant of God through Jesus Christ.

Healing is the will of Jesus
A man with leprosy came to Jesus for healing (Matthew 8:2-3). He knew that Jesus could heal, but he had a doubt whether Jesus would heal him. This is the same doubt that many of us are faced with today. He told Jesus, 'Lord, if you are willing, you can make me clean'. Jesus reached out his hand and touched the man. 'I am willing', he said 'Be clean!' Immediately he was cured of his leprosy. Jesus heals today. In fact during Jesus' earthly ministry one-third of His time spent in the healing ministry.

Healing is the sign of the Messiah
Isaiah prophesied that when the Messiah would come, these signs will accompany Him – the blind will see, the deaf will hear, the lame walk and the dumb speak (Isaiah 35:4-6). When Jesus came this prophecy was fulfilled. John had introduced Jesus as the Lamb of God that takes away the sins of the world. But when he was alone and shut up in prison, he had doubts and sent his messengers to ask Jesus if he was indeed the awaited Messiah. But at that time prophecy has being fulfilled by the ministry of Jesus. The Lord told his messengers to 'go and tell John what they have seen and heard': "The blind receive sight, the lame walk, those who have leprosy are cured, the deaf hear, the dead are raised, and the good news is preached to the poor", Luke 7:21-22.

Jesus' great compassion and love
God hates to see us suffering. His heart of compassion is moved

greatly when we suffer. This is revealed in the life and the ministry of our Lord. "Jesus went through all the towns and villages, teaching in their synagogues, preaching the good news of the kingdom and healing every disease and sickness. When He saw the crowds, He had compassion on them, because they were harassed and helpless, like sheep without a shepherd", Matthew 9:35-36. "When Jesus landed and saw a large crowd, He had compassion on them and healed their sick", Matthew 14:14. (See also Matthew 20:34). When we are hurt, He is also hurt because we are part of His body on the earth.

The Divine Exchange

Healing is in the Atonement. We can expect healing because it has been purchased for us on Calvary. A wonderful divine exchange was made at the cross, a transaction that took place through the sacrificial death of Jesus. He removed from us all our sins and all our sicknesses and diseases, and in their place we received His salvation, forgiveness and healing. Jesus accepted our punishment and He paid the price for our sins. Jesus was punished that we might be forgiven, Jesus was wounded that we might be healed. The following scriptures support these facts. "Surely he took up our infirmities and carried our sorrows....but he was pierced for our transgressions, he was crushed for our iniquities; the punishment that brought us peace was upon him, and by his wounds we are healed", Isaiah 53:4-5. "He himself bore our sins in his body on the tree, so that we might die to sins and live for righteousness; by his wounds you have been healed", 1 Peter 2:24. "Christ redeemed us from the curse of the law by becoming a curse for us, for it is written: 'Curse is everyone who is hung on a tree'", Galatians 3:13. Divine healing is part of the great atonement of Jesus Christ. As the psalmist says, let us bless God and not forget all his benefits!

Promises of Healing in the Word of God

The Bible is full of promises by God, to answer our prayers. These promises are God's provisions by which we have to access His grace by faith. When we need healing, we should go to God's Word and build healing scriptures into our spirit. Our body is healed as the Word becomes life to us. "for they are life to those who find them and health to man's whole body", Proverbs 4:22. Jesus urges us repeatedly to ask and receive (take) in John chapters 14, 15 and 16. Jesus exhorts His disciples in Matthew 18:19, saying, "Again, I tell you that if two of you on earth agree about anything you ask for, it will be done for you by my Father in heaven".

How to Receive Healing

Believe and apply the Word for oneself

The Word of God is able to heal. Psalm 107:21 says, "He sent forth his word and healed them...". We have faith in what God has said, we believe Him. The Bible says, "...faith comes by hearing, and hearing by the word of God", Romans 10:17 NKJV. So let us believe God's promises from His Word. (See also Proverbs 4:20-23; Isaiah 53:4-5; Matthew 13:15,21-22; 1 Peter 2:24). Hear the Word, receive it by faith, believe and stand on it.

Call for the elders of the church

Jesus confirmed divine healing by healing all who came to Him as He walked the byways of Israel. The lasting ordinance that we must do the same is commanded in James 5:14-15. The elders or leaders of the church should be people of faith, people who know how to pray the prayer of faith. Praying with the faith that it is the will of God to heal is the prayer of faith. The prayer of faith will save (heal) the sick.

The prayer of agreement

Jesus said, "I tell you the truth whatever you bind on earth will be bound in heaven, and whatever you loose on earth will be loosed in heaven. Again, I tell you that if two of you on earth agree about anything you ask for, it will be done for you by my Father in heaven", Matthew 18:18-19. When two or three believers get together in Jesus' name, He is there too. And if they ask anything and agree in prayer, it is done (Matthew 18:20; John 15:7). It is a knitting or yoking together in prayer, based on the Scripture. When two pray with such a heartfelt desire for healing, that prayer of agreement will heal the sick. Jesus said that in prayer of agreement we can ask for anything and that includes healing.

Laying on of hands

Jesus instructed the believers that 'they will lay hands on the sick, and they will recover' (Mark 16:18). We can receive healing through people of faith by actually lay their hands on the sick person and pray, and believe we are healed as a result. One way to pray is, 'Father, in Jesus' name I ask you for a manifestation of healing' or to command 'body I command you to be healed in Jesus' name.' Hebrews 6:2 tells us that, healing by the laying on of hands is one of the fundamental doctrines.

Claiming promises or confession of our faith

Scriptures are filled with God's promises. This involves more than just saying 'I am healed' a few times. We have to dedicate ourselves our time and our efforts to receiving the very best God has to offer. (See below 'confessions of healing'). "I tell you the truth, if anyone says to this mountain, 'Go throw yourself into the sea,' and does not doubt in his heart but believes that what he says will happen, it will be done for him", Mark 11:23. Our faith has to be in two places –

in our heart and in our mouth – believing and speaking. "For it is with your heart that you believe..., and it is with your mouth that you confess...", Romans 10:10.

Partaking of the Lord's Supper

This is a fundamental way to help receive healing and this has been my own experience. When we receive the Body and the Blood of our Lord Jesus, we should be keenly aware that we are standing on the Blood Covenant of the New Testament and acting according to the Word of God. (1 Corinthians 11:23-30). Let us remember that Jesus paid a high price for both forgiveness of sins and the healing of our body. By receiving Holy Communion, we are reminding ourselves that we partake of everything Jesus' sacrifice has provided – salvation, healing, peace, wholeness, strength and prosperity.

Have faith in the name of Jesus

Jesus' name carries all the authority of Jesus Himself. "Then Peter said, 'Silver or gold I do not have but what I have I give you. In the name of Jesus Christ of Nazareth, walk", Acts 3:6. When Peter spoke in Jesus' name, it was as if Jesus was speaking. He didn't pray for the man at the gate called Beautiful. He spoke words of faith – In Jesus' name. In the same way and with the same authority, we can speak to the affliction that attacks our bodies.

Confessions of Healing

There are many promises concerning divine healing. Let us equip ourselves with these promises and pray claiming them and believing that God will grant our request. Confession is based on faith. Faith comes from the person of Jesus (Hebrews 12:2), His words (Romans 10:17) and from His works (John 10:38; John 14:11). Proverbs

18:21 says, "Life and death are in the power of the tongue". Divine healing can be manifested instantaneously or progressively.

The Word of God spoken in faith will save us from our infirmities:

You are the Lord that heals me (Exodus 15:26).

You take sickness away from the midst of me and the number of my days you fulfil (Exodus 23:25-26).

You take away all sickness from me (Deuteronomy 7:15).

I am redeemed from the curse of the law (Deuteronomy 28:15-68 and Galatians 3:13).

You heal all my diseases (Psalm 103:3).

You sent your Word and healed me and delivered me from destruction (Psalm 107:20).

I shall not die, but live and declare the works of the Lord (Psalm 118:17).

With long life you will satisfy me and show me your salvation (Psalm 91:16).

Your words are life to me and health to all my flesh (Proverbs 4:22).

Surely you have born my sicknesses and carried my pains. Jesus Himself took my infirmities and bore my sicknesses (Isaiah 53:4 and Matthew 8:17).

With His stripes I am healed, by His stripes I was healed (Isaiah 53:5 and 1 Peter 2:24).

The life of Jesus is made manifest in my mortal flesh (2 Corinthians 4:11).

The same spirit that raised up Christ from the dead quickens my mortal body (Romans 8:11).

When hands are laid on me, I recover (Mark 16:18). I call my body healed/ whole/ strong (Joel 3:10 and Romans 4:17). Because I believe that Jesus Christ shed His blood for the remission of my sins and now they no longer exist. I believe He bore stripes for my physical healing. By faith I take full advantage of the benefits He paid for.

Hindrances to Healing

God has made it simple for us to receive healing. However, certain things can hinder us from receiving our healing. Here are a few reasons why healing is not manifested in some situations:

Not exercising our faith – Faith is essential for healing. Without faith it is impossible to please God (Hebrews 11:6). God cannot heal in an atmosphere of unbelief. Jesus could not do any mighty work in His hometown because of the unbelief of the people. "He could not do any miracles there, except lay his hands on a few people and heal them. And he was amazed at their lack of faith", Mark 6:5-6. We must walk by faith.

Doubt and fear – Fear is one of the everpresent companions of illness. Fear may come, but it need not overcome. "What I feared has come upon me; what I dreaded has happened to me", Job 3:25. If we are filled with the fear that we will not be healed or recover from our affliction then this can be a great hindrance to receive healing. Fear is a favourite weapon of Satan and he uses it in times of sickness to prevent children of God from receiving healing. We must believe in God and His word by faith, and doubt not.

Looking to man rather than to Jesus' work on Calvary – Although we should use the help of medical expertise (they are working for the same end result), we should not replace the Word of God and the provision of divine healing with that help. All kinds of people came to Jesus for healing (Mark 5:25-34). The first step of faith, will lead to greater blessings. Jesus wants us to be saved and healthy, so He purchased our salvation and healing with His own death on the cross.

Practising sin – When we practise sin it reaps corruption in our lives (Galatians 6:8). When we confess our sins 1 John 1:9 says that God is faithful and just to forgive us from our sins and to cleanse us from all iniquity.

Pride – Pride hinder divine healing and hence we must walk in love and humility. "God opposes the proud but gives grace to the humble", James 4:6b. Yes, we walk in love toward God and toward our fellow man.

Lack of knowledge – We must not lack the knowledge of God's will for healing. Be filled with the knowledge of God's Word and will, "my people are destroyed from lack of knowledge", Hosea 4:6; Colossians 1:9.

Unforgiveness – Mark 11:25-26 show us the importance of forgiving others in order to receive forgiveness, and so that our prayers are not hindered. We who have received such great grace and mercy should extend it to others. Healing is something that has to be received and it is hard to receive if our heart is full of bitterness and unforgiveness, it will hinder us from receiving our healing and anything else from God.

Concluding Remarks

God can heal through natural and supernatural means. God created the body to heal itself and some of the natural means of receiving healing are through adequate rest, balanced diet, regular exercise, sufficient sleep, proper or regulated work. Medication can help in many cases. The natural means of healing work towards the same end result. Remember that our ultimate source of healing is in what Jesus did on the cross – He bore our sicknesses and carried our pains, and by His stripes we were healed (Isaiah 53:4-5).

Divine healing is not just a blessing, it is our covenant right as a born-again child of God. Healing belongs to us because of Jesus' redemptive work at Calvary. The scriptural evidence for it is over-whelming and convincing without a shadow of doubt. God is no respecter of persons (Acts 10:34) and He never changes (Malachi 3:6). God's Word is God speaking to us. For instance God's announcement: 'I am the LORD, who heals you'. Accordingly, "He sent forth his word and healed them", (Psalm 107:20). Seven blessings of His covenant are revealed to us by His redemptive names which include 'Jehovah - Rapha' (The LORD our healer). His covenants including the covenant of healing are given because of His mercy. We know, it is God's will to heal us because "the steadfast love of the Lord never ceases and his compassion never fails", Lamentations 3:22.

During the earthly ministry of our Lord Jesus, He was 'moved with compassion and healed all that had need of healing'. Healing is a gift, like salvation, already paid for at Calvary. All we need to do is access it by faith. 'Faith begins where the will of God is known'. Christ is our healer. "Jesus Christ is the same yesterday, today and forever", Hebrews 13:8.

Let us conclude this study in the words of B. Jones, "As we increases in our knowledge of God's will; as we walk in faith, not ignorant of Satan's devices; as we are obedient to God's word and to the leading of the Holy Spirit; and as we walk in the love of God and in humility of heart, we will be in a wonderful position to walk in Divine health and healing"[1].

Chapter 22

THE KINGDOM OF GOD

But he [Jesus] said, "I must preach the good news of the kingdom of God to the other towns also, because that is why I was sent."
(Luke 4:42-44)

Introduction

The kingdom of God was a central theme of Jesus' teaching. Jesus' ministry started with the proclamation of the message that 'the kingdom of God is at hand' (Matthew 4:17; Mark 1:15). To proclaim the kingdom was an obligation that was laid up on Him (Luke 4:43). It was the message of the kingdom that He went through the town and villages of Galilee preaching, and His message was accompanied by a demonstration of the power of the kingdom.

"And Jesus went about all Galilee, teaching in their synagogues, preaching the gospel of the kingdom, and healing all kinds of sickness and all kinds of disease among the people", Matthew 4:23 NKJV.

The Gospels use two phrases, the kingdom of God and the kingdom of heaven – and their meaning is exactly the same. The two expressions are interchangeable. The phrase 'kingdom of God' occurs 68 times in ten different New Testament books, 'while kingdom of heaven' occurs only 32 times, and only in the Gospel of Matthew. In answer to the rich young ruler's question concerning eternal life (Matthew 19:16-24), Christ uses the phrases 'kingdom of God' and 'kingdom of heaven' because they refer to the same thing.

Kingdom of God Explained

The kingdom of heaven is not a geographic location. In the New Testament, the kingdom of God is the sovereignty, the lordship, the rule and the reign of God. It is a spiritual realm where God rules and reigns, where we share in his eternal life.

The kingdom of God is good news! It was good news to the 1st century Jews because they had been awaiting the coming of the promised Messiah ever since the Babylonian captivity. It is good news for us today because it means freedom from slavery to sin and selfishness.

Consequently, the kingdom of God is here and now because we can enter into that kingdom when we trust in Christ as Saviour and the Holy Spirit come to indwell the hearts of believers.

Yet it is also in the future because Jesus will return to reign over a perfect kingdom where sin and evil no longer exist. As such, it represents mankind's hope for the future, for God's kingdom will one day fill the whole earth.

Characteristics of the Kingdom

Jesus said, "the kingdom of God is within you", Luke 17:21. The kingdom of God within us is characterised by the rule, the presence and the authority and power of the King.

The rule of the King: Jesus' call to the hearers of his message was always a call to 'follow' him. Romans 10:9-10 tell us that our salvation experience begins with a confession of Jesus as 'Lord'. Jesus instructed that we were to "seek first the kingdom of God and his righteousness" (Matthew 6:33). That means to first have the rule of the king operating in our lives, and then to extend that rule through our lives. So our entering into the kingdom means our being brought into a life in which God rules over all, His will is truly and joyfully done, and all the blessedness that reigns in heaven finds its counterpart here below. As it is written, "the kingdom of God is righteousness, and peace and joy in the Holy Spirit", Romans 14:17.

The presence of the King: When we come into the kingdom, the King comes to make his home in us through his Spirit. He now indwells us and we can know fellowship with the Father, the Son and the Holy Spirit (2 Corinthians 13:14; 1 John 1:3). And through Christ, we have access to the Most Holy Place, the throne room of God (Hebrews 10:19-22).

The authority and power of the King: A Roman centurion once recognised that Jesus carried the authority of heaven and could with a word heal his servant. Explaining that 'I too am a man under authority', the centurion accurately understood that Jesus' authority came from the fact that he was perfectly submitted to God the Father's authority. Colossians 1:13 tells us that people who have received Jesus have been rescued from the dominion or authority of darkness and brought 'into the kingdom of the Son He loves'. As we come under the rule of God, the authority of the kingdom not only flows into our lives, it also flows through us. As heir of the kingdom and co-heirs with Christ, we are seated with him in heavenly places. From our position in Christ, we pray for God's kingdom to come (Matthew 6:10), we proclaim the good news of the kingdom so that others too may enter in, and we labour for the expansion of the kingdom of God on earth for "the kingdom of God is not in word but in power", 1 Corinthians 4:20 NKJV.

A life in the presence and the will and the power of God is now available to all who would follow the King.

The Parables of Jesus about the Kingdom of God.

A parable is an earthly story with a heavenly purpose, a story or illustration set in everyday life that illustrates a profound moral or spiritual truth. Jesus told many parables in order to make truth of the kingdom of God clearer:

- The sower – (Matthew 13:3-8; Mark 4:4-8; Luke 8:5-8)
- The tares (the weeds) – (Matthew 13:24-30)
- The mustard seed – (Matthew 13:31-32; Mark 4:30-32; Luke 13:18-19)
- The leaven (the yeast) – (Matthew 13:33; Luke 13:20-21)
- The hidden treasure – (Matthew 13:44)
- The pearl of great price – (Matthew 13:45-46)
- The drag net (fishing net) – (Matthew 13:47-50)
- The growing seed – (Mark 4:26-29)

Parable after parable served to illustrate the kingdom of God. Its invitations, its demands, its paramount importance are consistently stressed. They explain what the kingdom is really like as opposed to our expectations of it.

In Matthew 13:44-46 Jesus explained, the kingdom of heaven is more valuable than anything else we can have, and the person must be willing to give up everything to obtain it. The man who discovered the treasure in the field stumbled upon it by accident but knew its value when he found it. The merchant was earnestly searching for the pearl of great value, and, when he found it, he sold everything he had to purchase it. The kingdom involves a separation and a division between men. This is notably shown in the parables of the tares and the drag net.

Jesus saying to us in the parable of the mustard seed that we must serve and witness in our own situations, and from each small endeavour and tiny beginning the kingdom of God grows until the kingdoms of the earth finally become the "kingdom of our Lord".

Hunger and Seek after the Kingdom of God

The kingdom of God is to be accepted by men on earth as it is in heaven. Consequently, we are urged to seek the kingdom (Matthew 6:33; Luke 12:31). Jesus categorically stated that a man could only enter the kingdom through the new birth (John 3:1-7; see chapter 1: 'The New Birth'). Primarily, it means we are to seek the salvation that is inherent in the kingdom of God because it is of greater value than all the world's riches. The first call of the kingdom is to 'repent and believe' – to turn back to the King and trust Him – resulting in the new birth. At the new birth, the believer enters into a new relationship with God and a new way of living, giving rise to new, the fruit of a changed life (Matthew 3:1-2; 4:17).

Seeking the kingdom of God means making Jesus the Lord and King of our lives. That is to make the kingdom the object of our entire endeavour. We are implored to press into the kingdom (Matthew 11:12; Luke 16:16). To enter the kingdom is worth any sacrifice. The kingdom is nothing less than heaven and nothing less than life.

Jesus said to seek first the kingdom of God in His Sermon on the Mount (Matthew 6:33). We are to seek the things of God as a priority over the things of the world. As we take care of God's business as a priority – living in close fellowship with Him, walking in obedience to Him, and sharing the good news of the kingdom with others – then He will take care of our business as He promised. Jesus taught that our focus should be away from this world and placed upon the things of God's kingdom.

Entry to the Kingdom of God

We enter the kingdom of God when we are born-again, and we are then part of that kingdom for eternity. It is a relationship 'born of the Spirit' (John 3:5), and we have confidence and assurance that it is so because the Spirit bears witness with our spirit (Romans 8:16).

Furthermore, it speaks of the kingdom of heaven come to earth, and our entering into it in power, as the disciples did at Pentecost. God's manifested presence with us without ceasing; God's blessed rule and dominion over us established, so that His heavenly will is done in us and through us; God's mighty power descending upon us, so that through us Christ can do His work of saving souls. We can only enter by faith. It was Jesus who from heaven gave the disciples their abundant entrance into the kingdom; it is He who still by his Holy Spirit leads each one of us into His kingdom. We can trust Him to bring us in. However before we can enter the kingdom, it must first enter into us; that is we must receive the kingdom by faith. It implies two things: There is one who gives, and another who accepts. What is dark and evil within must first be cast out; what is of God must fill our being;

for that which is born of God alone can inherit the kingdom and its heavenly life.

In the Gospels the kingdom is spoken of as the gift and the work of God, as that which is given, as that which has come by the action of God towards man. Jesus said to his disciples that it was the Father's good pleasure to give them the kingdom (Luke 12:32). However, it is a gift to be received and a work to participate in. Consequently, He also said that the kingdom must be received (Mark 10:15; Luke 18:17) and entered into (Matthew 5:20, 18:3, 19:23; Mark 10:23-25).

So, while the kingdom is entirely given, is entirely the gift of God, Jesus lays down certain very definite conditions to fully partaking in the life of the kingdom:

- No man can enter the kingdom without child-like faith (Matthew 18:3) – We must accept God with the humility and faith of a child.

- No man can partake in kingdom life without the forgiving spirit (Matthew 18:23-35) – We must forgive as God forgives and treat men as God treats men.

- No man can partake in the kingdom life without a certain attitude to his fellow-men (Matthew 25:31-46).

- If a man has entered the kingdom, he has access to and should demonstrate love (*agape*) in action.

- When one enters the kingdom we can bear the fruit of righteousness. The reason for this is that righteousness stems from our new nature in Christ, therefore we are able to practice righteousness in our actions (2 Corinthians 5:21).

Hindrances to the Entry to the Kingdom of God

Anything that is more important to us than God, for example, the accumulation of wealth, can be a hindrance to entry to the kingdom. The Bible says that it is very hard for a rich man to enter the kingdom of God (Matthew 19:23; Mark 10: 23-25; Luke 18:24). Riches can encourage a false independence in a man, make him feel he can buy his way into or buy his way out of anything. Riches are not a sin, in fact they can be a blessing. But if the love of them exceeds the love of God they are a very great danger and threat to a man's entry to the kingdom. If a man put his hand to the plough, and looks back, he is not partaking in the kingdom life (Luke 9:61).

Lack of forgiveness blocks access to the kingdom and to its marvellous power (see chapter 5: 'The Joy of Forgiveness'). If we want to experience the life and power of the kingdom flowing in our own life, it is absolutely imperative that we forgive.

Concluding Remarks

The kingdom of God and the kingdom of heaven are synonymous to the kingdom. The parables of Matthew 13 describe the course and character of the kingdom. We ought to be diligent, with open hearts and exercised minds, to give honest and ready reception to the Word of God.

The King will come back to be vindicated. He will rule and reign, and His kingdom will extend from the sea to sea and from the river to the ends of the earth (Psalm 72).

We read in Matthew 5:3, the kingdom belongs to the poor in spirit – When a man realises his own utter helplessness and inadequacy, and submits his ignorance to God's wisdom, his weakness to God's power, his sin to God's mercy, then he enters the kingdom of God. In the 'Sermon on the Mount', Jesus outlines eight primary characteristics of people who receive the rule of God's kingdom (Matthew 5:3-10):

"Blessed are the poor in spirit, for theirs is the kingdom of heaven" (v 3)

Blessed are those who mourn... (v 4)

Blessed are the meek... (v 5)

Blessed are those who hunger and thirst for righteousness... (v 6)

Blessed are the merciful... (v 7)

Blessed are the pure in heart... (v 8)

Blessed are the peacemakers... (v 9)

Blessed are those who are persecuted..." (v 10)

These Beatitudes (blessings) contrast kingdom values (what is eternal) with worldly values (what is temporary).

The Holy Spirit is the One who brings power of the kingdom into a person's life and must be received (John 7:37-38; Acts 1:3-8). The kingdom of God is a spiritual reality that occupies one's life, overrules one's affairs, and is expressed through one's life, love, and service. Kingdom people seek different blessings and benefits, and they have different attitudes – they reflect the humility and self-sacrifice of Jesus, our King.

Chapter 23

THE Second Coming OF JESUS

For as often as you eat this bread and drink this cup,
you proclaim the Lord's death till He comes.
(1 Corinthians 11:26 NKJV)

Introduction

One of the foundations of the Christian faith is Jesus' Second Coming. Yet, it is a widely misunderstood and debated topic. In this chapter, I shall endeavour to simplify this theme. Jesus is coming again. This is the unequivocal testimony of the Bible. It is something that all evangelical, Bible-believing Christians agree with and it is something that should give us enormous hope. The doctrine of the Second Coming tells us that God is concerned about violence, injustice, strife, conflict, sin, suffering and wickedness in the world. And Jesus is coming to put an end to it all. The kingdom of God has come through Him and the time will come when this present evil age will come to an end. The Second Coming of Christ is something that brings hope and encouragement to us all.

Brief Description of the End of the Age

People today often call out with God's prophet, "What shall be the end of these things?", Daniel 12:8 NKJV. The Lord's description of the end of the age provides part of the answer in Matthew 24. The disciples had asked Jesus a question, "What will be the sign of your coming, and of the end of the age?", v 2. Jesus described the general signs of the present age, vv 4-14, and the second by naming the special signs of the end of the age, vv 15-51. The warning signs of His coming to reign as Son of Man are 'the abomination that causes desolation'", v 15 and the great tribulation, "...there will be great distress, unequalled from the beginning of the world until now – and never to be equalled again", v 21; (also Mark 13:14-23; Luke 21:5-24).

The Second Coming refers to Jesus' return to earth itself, conquering Satan (Revelation 16:15-17, 17:14) and reclaiming God's kingdom with His saints (1 Thessalonians 3:13; Zechariah 14:5; Jude v 14). Jesus himself foretold of His return in Matthew 24 and 25. In these two chapters, He goes into great details about the events leading up to the time of His return:

The imminence of His coming (Matthew 24:32-33).

The certainty of His coming (Matthew 24:34-36).

The Lord Jesus gives assurance, firstly, that Jewish nation will exist when He returns.

He gives assurance secondly that He will return to deliver and re-gather His people.

The expectation of His coming (Matthew 24:42-44; 25:13).

Therefore, we are required to exercise constant vigilance (Hebrews 10:37).

Jesus' Coming will be Personal, Public, Audible, Sudden and Visible

"For as the lightning comes from the east and flashes to the west, so also will the coming of the Son of Man be", Matthew 24:27 NKJV. "Men of Galilee", they said, "why do you stand here looking into the sky? This same Jesus, who has been taken from you into heaven, will come back in the same way you have seen him going into heaven", Acts 1:11. Let us be very clear – Jesus is coming personally and physically. Just as personally, as He was here in his first coming. The Bible says that a trumpet will sound (1 Corinthians 15:52; 1 Thessalonians 4:16) and every eye will see Jesus (Revelation 1:7). It will not be in secret. It will be something that no one can deny!

Jesus will come in glory

Jesus' return will be glorious and triumphant. "At that time the sign of the Son of Man will appear in the sky and all the nations of the earth will mourn. They will see the Son of Man coming on the clouds of the sky with power and great glory. And he will send his angels with a loud trumpet call, and they will gather his elect from the four winds, from one end of the heavens to the other", Matthew 24:30-31. When Jesus came the first time, He laid aside His glory. He laid aside His right to be recognised as God. He laid aside His right to be worshipped (Philippians 2:5-8). "Therefore God exalted him to the highest place and gave him the name that is above every name, that at the name of Jesus every knee should bow, in heaven and on earth and under the earth, and every tongue confess that Jesus Christ is Lord, to the glory of God the Father", Philippians 2:9-11. Jesus is currently at the right hand of His Father, reigning in glory. When He comes again, He will not lay aside that glory.

When Jesus comes again, nobody will be able to deny that He came, and that He is God Himself. He will demonstrate that sin and death have been conquered completely and He rules. Jesus reigns and every single person on this earth owes Him worship.

Jesus will come in judgement

The Bible declares that Jesus will be the final judge of the world (John 5:22; Acts 10:42; 2 Timothy 4:1). Jesus, speaking of Himself in Matthew 25:31-32, "When the Son of Man comes in his glory, and all the angels with him, he will sit on his throne in heavenly glory. All the nations will be gathered before him, and he will separate the people from one another as a shepherd separates the sheep from the goats".

When Jesus comes, the dead will be resurrected to stand before the Lord. Peter describes the day of Christ's return as "the day of judgement and destruction of ungodly men", 2 Peter 3:7b. All will be judged – the unrighteous will be send to everlasting punishment and the righteous will live forever. The Bible says, "He will punish those who do not know God and do not obey the gospel of our Lord Jesus. They will be punished with everlasting destruction and shut out from the presence of the Lord and from the majesty of his power on the day he comes to be glorified in his holy people and to be marvelled at among all those who have believed. This includes you, because you believed our testimony to you.", 2 Thessalonians 1:8-10.

Jesus described hell as the place where "their worm does not die, and the fire is not quenched", Mark 9:48 NKJV. Revelation chapter 20 talks about hell being thrown into the lake of fire but that does not mean it will cease to exist (Mark 9:43; Revelation 14:9-11). Hell is very real unending terror, and it is the fate of those who do not run to Jesus. For those who do give their life to Jesus, their destination is the new heaven and the new earth. When Christians die now, they go to heaven to be with the Lord (Luke 23:43; Philippians 1:23). But the current heaven is merely a waiting room. The current state is just temporary. When Jesus comes, there will be a new heaven and a new earth where we shall live (Revelation 21:1-4).

Jesus' Coming Will Usher in a New Age

Let us be clear that things will not be the same when Jesus comes. Jesus' coming will bring unprecedented change. Jesus frequently referred to the age to come. And we experience something of that age now, but when Jesus comes again the old order will pass away and He will make all things new. Revelation chapter 21 reveals to us that God has written the final chapter, and it is about true fulfilment and eternal joy to those who love him. At the end of the age Satan is defeated, sin is vanquished, the curse is removed, no more tears or sorrow, the earth is made new, death is defeated (no more death). A new heaven and earth will be formed. And the righteous in Christ will live with God and His Christ forever.

We do not know when Jesus will come

"No one knows about that day or hour, not even the angels in heaven, nor the Son, but only the Father. Be on guard! Be alert! You do not know when that time will come", Mark 13:32-33. The Bible teaches us that anyone who claims to be able to predict Jesus' return is either seriously misled or seriously misleading because we cannot know. Some say, what about Jesus' claim that He would come soon? "But do not forget this one thing, dear friends: With the Lord a day is like a thousand years, and a thousand years are like a day. The Lord is not slow in keeping his promise, as some understand slowness. He is patient with you, not wanting anyone to perish, but everyone to come to repentance", 1 Peter 3:8-9. God's Word is trustworthy and He is the God of all history – past, present and future. Jesus has not come back yet because there are people who need to turn from sin and turn to Jesus – He is patient and wants no one to perish. This shows us God's unchanging heart, but Jesus' return is imminent.

Jesus' Coming Will Be Preceded by Signs

In Olivet Discourse (Matthew 24; Mark 13; Luke 21), Jesus indicated a number of signs which would appear, preceding His return:

A prevalence of deception (Matthew 24: 4),

Wars and rumours of wars (Mark 13:7),

Famines and earthquakes (Mark 13:8),

Preaching of the gospel to all nations (Mark 13:10),

Great tribulation (Mark 13: 7-8, 19-20),

False prophets working signs and wonders (Mark 13:22),

Signs in the heavens (Mark 13:24-25),

Nations will rise against nation and kingdom against kingdom (Luke 21:10).

Also: The coming of the man of sin and rebellion (2 Thessalonians 2:1-18),

The salvation of Israel (Romans 11:12, 25-26),

These signs are also recorded in Matthew 24, are linked with events described in the book of Revelation.

The Rapture

The rapture is a belief that believers will be 'caught up' with Jesus although some discount the idea of the rapture altogether. The word 'rapture' means 'caught, away, up', in Greek. Paul, in first Thessalonians 4:17 tells us that the Lord will come down from heaven, with a loud command, with the voice of the archangel and with the trumpet call of God. At this time, 'the dead in Christ will rise first' and those who are still alive will be 'caught up...in the clouds to meet the Lord in the air'. The event will happen quickly. The Bible says, it will happen in 'the twinkling of an eye'. "Then they will see the Son of Man coming in the clouds with great power and glory. And then He will send His angels, and gather together His elect from the four winds, from the farthest part of earth to the farthest part of heaven", Mark 13:26-27 NKJV.

We should be ready

It is very important that we are ready when our Lord returns. "... So then, dear friends, since you are looking forward to this, make every effort to be found spotless, blameless and at peace with him", 2 Peter 3:10-14. The question is, are we preparing for our eternal future? It will be radically different – a place free from sin. So what is our attitude to sin now? A place in the presence of the Lord! So are we people, who enjoy His presence now? So are we worshipping Him now? This world is not our home – it will pass away. Sin has no future. We need to examine ourselves and do not let sin take control of us.

Wiersbe summed up well in his commentary on Matthew's Gospel chapter 25:

'When Jesus Christ returns, it will be a time of separation: the wise will be separated from the foolish, the faithful servants from the unfaithful, the blessed (sheep) from the cursed (goats).

His coming also means evaluation. As we wait for the Lord to return, we must invest our lives and earn dividends for His glory. Christ gives us opportunities that match our abilities. The key is faithfulness (1 Corinthians 4:2).

"When Christ returns, it will be a time of commendation. We will be surprised to learn about ministries we performed that we thought were insignificant but that He will reward"[1].

We should be looking forward to Jesus' Coming

In 1 Corinthians 16:22, Paul uses a phrase, 'Maranatha', which means 'Come Lord.' And it should be a desire of us all. Paul says, "grown inwardly as we wait eagerly for...the redemption of our bodies", Romans 8:23. "Therefore you do not lack any spiritual gift as you eagerly wait for our Lord Jesus Christ to be revealed", 1 Corinthians 1:7. Are we ready? Are we eager? The Bible says that our citizenship is in heaven (Philippians 3:20). And we eagerly await a Saviour from there, the Lord Jesus Christ, who, by the power that enables him to bring everything under his control will transform our lowly bodies so that they will be like his glorious body", Philippians 3:20-21.

Every chapter in 1 Thessalonians ends with a reference to the Second Coming of Jesus Christ, and that the eager looking for His Second Coming is an evidence of salvation (1:9-10), a motivation for soul winning (2:17-20), and an encouragement for holy living (3:11-13). To be ready for Christ's coming, we as God's people must be sober and live in the light (5:23).

Concluding Remarks

Jesus is coming back. Christians must be given to 'wholesome thinking' (2 Peter 3:1). In 2 Peter chapter three, according to Brown, we find three attitudes regarding the return of Christ:

The world's attitude – People deliberately despise Christ's return (vv 3-7). Like Noah's contemporaries, they greet his message with blatant unbelief.

The Lord's attitude – He deliberately postpones His return (vv 8-10).

The Christian's attitude – We deliberately anticipate His return (vv 11-18). Believers prepare for their glorious future and 'speed its coming' (v 12) by holiness (vv 11,14), expectancy (v 13), watchfulness (v 17) and increasing maturity (v 18)[2].

We don't know the day or the hour, but Jesus is coming soon and unexpectedly. This is good news to those who trust Him. Soon means at any moment, and we must be ready for Him, always be prepared for His return. Unless we live in the light of the Lord's return, we are liable to be ashamed before Him at His Coming.

The book of Revelation ends with an urgent request:

'Come, Lord Jesus', 22:20

In a world of problem, persecution, evil, and immorality, Christ calls us to endure in our faith. Jesus alone forgives sin and will re-create the earth and bring lasting peace. "...I go to prepare a place for you. And if I go and prepare a place for you, I will come again and receive you to Myself; that where I am there you may be also", John 14:2-3 NKJV.

CONCLUSION

I pray this book has been a source of blessing to you. I recommend that you read and study it again and again, as exploring this vast mine of truth and making it real in your own life will enrich your spirit, soul and body. Jesus said that, "If you hold to my teaching, you are really my disciples. Then you will know the truth, and the truth will set you free", John 8:31b-32. The truth is not some statement of doctrine that we merely accepted once in the past; it has to be applied to every part of our daily lives. The truth – when we receive it and live by it – has the power to set us free to live life as God intended.

We must seek earnestly to love God, trust God and fear (have reverence for) God, and to learn to walk in his ways and in his truth. We must also learn to proclaim and share the truth with those that are seeking after God, and to protect the truth from those who oppose Christ by denying his deity and humanity. If this book has been helpful to you, please introduce others to the truths within and most of all to The Truth, which is Jesus Christ our Lord – and thereby help them too to embrace life to the full.

"And now, all glory to God, who is able to keep you from stumbling, and who will bring you into his glorious presence innocent of sin and with great joy. All glory to him, who alone is God our Saviour, through Jesus Christ our Lord. Yes, glory, majesty, power, and authority belong to him, in the beginning, now, and forevermore. Amen", Jude vv 24, 25 NLT.

Appendix 1

THE ROLE OF THE BIBLE IN EMBRACING LIFE TO THE FULL

In order to understand the importance of reading and studying the Bible for growing in our Christian lives, we need to understand the nature, purpose and workings of the Christian life. The essential nature of the Christian life is all about enjoying a restored right relationship with God our Father, through the Lord Jesus Christ and by the enabling for the Holy Spirit (Ephesians 1:3-14). Our old life was one of a wrong and broken relationships with God that resulted from sin. Sin, in its essence, is being self-centred rather than God-centred (Isaiah 53:6). However, our new life in Christ, as we truly embrace Jesus Christ as Lord, is one with God at the very centre, where He takes the highest place. When we become Christians, we did not sign up for a club, a society, a denomination or a church – we signed up for a person, the Lord Jesus (Philippians 3:7-11). Being a Christian by definition is being a follower of Christ. The essential purpose of the Christian life is to follow Christ in that relationship and to find our place in His purposes (Philippians 3:12-14), which involves making Him and His salvation known to the earth and seeing His kingdom established in our lives and that of others. The Christian life works when we use every God-given means to benefit from and enjoy all that Christ purchased for us at the cross and has been made available to us by His Spirit (Romans 8:31-32).

Once God is at the centre of our lives, then the Bible, God's written Word, must automatically also come to the centre of our lives. God and His Word are intrinsically linked (Psalm 138:2); Jesus is the personal Word of God, and the Bible is the written Word of God. We cannot grow in our knowledge of God except by growing in the knowledge and application of His Word. We cannot know what Jesus has purchased for us at the cross other than by knowing it from the Bible, made alive to us by the Holy Spirit. We cannot even properly know ourselves except by God's help through His Word. Furthermore, our love for Jesus is expressed and made real by our obedience to His Word (John 14:23). The Bible makes it clear that once Jesus has become the foundation, the Rock, of our lives, we grow and build on that foundation by living according to His Word, i.e. by hearing and doing what He says (Matthew 7:24-27). In the natural, we need food and nourishment to grow. In the Christian life, God's nourishment for us to grow is in His Word. The Bible is pure milk for the new and young believer, a staple of bread for daily living, and solid food for those who are mature (1 Peter 2:2-3; Matthew 4:4; Hebrews 5:11-14) – in other words, the Bible contains what we need to grow no matter what stage we are at in the Christian life.

Once we give the Bible its proper place in our lives, studying and applying it, then it can become to us all that it has promised to be. Some, by no means all, of these blessings and benefits are listed below:

- It reveals to us the nature, character and attributes of God, showing us the One we desire to know intimately and be like (John 5:39; Luke 24:27).

- It reveals God's calling and purposes for us in this life (Matthew 28:18-20).

- Living by it results in a growing revelation of Jesus and intimacy with Him (John 14:21).

- It reveals to us the will of God and thereby enables us to pray effectively (1 John 5:14-15).

- In living by it, we will be established and blessed (Psalm 1; Matthew 7:24-27; James 1:22-25).

- It washes and cleanses us (John 15:3; Ephesians 5:25-27).

- It ministers healing to us from God (Psalm 107:20; Proverbs 4:20-22).

- It accomplishes the purposes of God (Isaiah 55:10-11).

- It reveals our heart (Hebrews 4:12).

- It shows us who we are, by correcting our wrong thinking, character and behaviour, and revealing who we truly are in Christ Jesus (James 1:22-25).

- It teaches us all that God has promised us in Christ (2 Corinthians 1:20).

- It is able to save those who receive the Word of God (2 Timothy 3:14-15; James 1:21; 1 Peter 1:23).

- It instructs, corrects, reproves and trains us in righteousness, equipping us for every good work (2 Timothy 3:16-17).

- It directs us (Psalm 119:105).

As well as receiving these benefits of the Bible for ourselves, we also learn about our privilege, responsibility and capacity to pass these on to others (Matthew 10:7-8; 28:18-20).

In addition to teaching us by instruction, the Bible also teaches us powerfully by life examples. Seeing other people's experiences with God creates in us a desire for more and inspires us to pursue and enter into the same. The Bible is a window into the unknown. The Christian life is about reaching out far where we have never been before in our relationship with God and our journey with Him. The Bible informs us of what can be, motivating us to press on and lay hold of all that for which Christ laid hold of us (Philippians 3:12-14). Without the Word of God, it is easy to settle into a less-than-God-intended, man-made version of Christianity. However, through the Bible made alive to us by the Holy Spirit, God continually calls us into pursuing Him and His great purposes, and beckons us to reach out to become all that He has made us to be.

Appendix 2

REPENTANCE

Repentance means to have a change of mind that leads to a change of direction, or to turn from ourselves and our sin to God. Repentance is a basic and essential part of the message of the New Testament (Matthew 3:1-2, 4:17; Acts 3:19). Jesus taught, "unless you repent you too will all perish", Luke 13:3, 5.

The Significance of Repentance

Repentance conveys the meaning such as 'change one's mind for the better', 'to have a change of mind', and 'turning to God with true penitence'. It denotes an expression of sorrow for sin:

"Turn from your sins and turn to God, because the Kingdom of Heaven is near", Matthew 3:2 NLT.

"Now turn from your sins and turn to God, so you can be cleansed of your sins", Acts 3:19 NLT.

"Repent therefore of this your wickedness, and pray God if perhaps thought of your heart may be forgiven you", Acts 8:22 NKJV.

Genuine Repentance:

God demands genuine repentance – The kind of repentance which God demands from man is not a sentimental kind of sorrow or regret for sin, but a total change of mind and an intention to change for the better, a turning to God for His gracious forgiveness and mercy, and a departing from sin, showing proof of hatred for sin.

We read in the book of Joel, "Even now, declares the LORD, return to me with all your heart with fasting and weeping and mourning. Rend your heart and not your garments, Return to the LORD your God, for he is gracious and compassionate, slow to anger and abounding in love and he relents from sending calamity", 2:12-13. We see in the Gospel of Matthew, From that time Jesus began to preach and to say, "Repent for the kingdom of heaven is at hand", 4:17 NKJV. Also in Acts, Peter replied, "Repent and be baptised every one of you in the name of Jesus Christ for the forgiveness of your sins. And you will receive the gift of the Holy Spirit", 2:38.

Genuine repentance follows real conviction caused by the action of the Holy Spirit on conscience of the one repenting. God has many ways of dealing with man. According to His infinite wisdom, His methods vary from man to man. For example when Isaiah saw the vision of 'the Lord sitting upon a throne, high and lifted up', it was then that he cried saying, "woe is me, for I am undone! Because I am a man of unclean lips, And I dwell in the midst of a people of unclean lips; For mine eyes have seen the King, the LORD of hosts", Isaiah 6:1,5 NKJV. When Peter inspired by the Holy Spirit, preached to the multitude at Jerusalem on the day of Pentecost, they were cut to the heart, and said to Peter and the rest of the apostles, "Men and brethren, what shall we do?"..."Repent, and let every one of you be baptized in the name of Jesus Christ for the remission of sins", Acts 2:37-38.

The blessings that follow true repentance

True repentance enables God to change His mind and to revoke His judgement against the sinner (Joel 2:13-14; Jonah 3:9-10).

True repentance results in forgiveness of sins, remission of sins, and the cancelation of sins (Isaiah 55:7; Luke 24:47; Acts 3:19).

True repentance is the first step towards receiving Christ and the gift of the Holy Spirit (Acts 2:38; Acts 3:19-20).

True repentance of one sinner brings joy to the angels of God in heaven (Luke 15:7, 10).

True repentance leads to the gift of eternal life (Acts 11 18).

In Luke 15:11-32, Jesus tells the parable of the prodigal (or reckless) son, who leaves his father to go to a far off country where he squanders his inheritance. When he reached the point of desperation, 'he came to his senses' and returned "to his father and said to him, 'Father I have sinned against heaven and against you'", v 17-21. He had sinned against God, he had sinned against others, and he had sinned against himself. He had fought against his conscience, defiled his body and wounded his soul. Despite all these, his father's heart towards him was one of 'compassion', and his response was 'let us have a feast and celebrate' because he had his son back (v 23). The father's ear was opened to his honest confession and the father's hand was outstretched to him with the best robe, the son's ring, and the fattened calf. This parable ends with the father's statement, "But we had to celebrate and be glad, because this brother of yours was dead and is alive again; he was lost and is found" (v 32).

Appendix 3

MY TESTIMONY

It was on April fool's day in 1958 that my father died prematurely, having fallen from a coconut tree. I was barely eighteen years old and my whole world died with him. But God opened way for me to come to England in 1959 to begin a career. It took me eight solid years to raise enough money to go back and visit my hometown Venmony in Kerala. In the course of my four-week visit I got married to Mary. Having lived alone in England, I had very little knowledge in raising a family. As a result I made many mistakes on the way. The arrival of our baby daughter Helen, two years after our marriage was a great joy and helped in building our relationship. In 1974 we had an added blessing through the arrival of our son Paul. We slowly learned by trial and error how to be good parents.

As time went on we both admitted that there was something, a vital ingredient, missing from our lives. Though we both were brought up in Christian homes and attended church every Sunday, we kept Jesus in a corner of our hearts. This was the problem. Major parts of our hearts were filled with other things, like how to get a better job, collect more qualifications, how to make our home more attractive, how to get the approval of others and so on. In 1986, we jointly made a decision to rededicate ourselves to the Lord and give Jesus the centre place in our lives. This was the best thing we have ever done and it was a real turning point for us, marked by getting baptised in water and being filled with the Holy Spirit. From then on we got more involved in serving the Lord in our local church especially in the healing ministry and it brought us great joy to see people set free.

In 1991, I underwent a back operation which went totally wrong. It left me disabled and forced me to retire from my highly paid job at the London University of Greenwich. Did my world fall apart this time? As He promised He held me in the palms of His hands. As I look back, I can see that God's work never ceased – whether able bodied or disabled, God used us to help and minister to a large number of people and see them set free in every walk of life in England, Dubai, India, and Germany.

In 1996 we went to Kerala with a view to settle back there for good. But God had other plans for us. Though we went for a quiet life, we were busier than ever before. God wonderfully led us to be instrumental in building His kingdom for three and a half years. We got very much involved in the local church in working among the needy and the poor. Apart from preaching the Word of God and evangelising, we had opportunities to help to construct church buildings, help to train pastors, and nurses, helped with house renovations and extensions, assisted in providing water and electricity supplies and more. When the work assigned was over, the order from above unexpectedly came at the beginning of year 2000, asking us to return back to England to support our children in their walk with the Lord and ministry. It is interesting to recall that God gave me a dream three nights consecutively, about preaching the Word, prior to going to India.

In obedience to God's leading we came to live in Newcastle in the month of June 2000. Having tasted and seen that the Lord is good, I realised that Jesus Christ demands our service to Him in the area of evangelism and pastoral care. Whatever the cost, our personal commitment matters most to God. Within the first year of our stay in Newcastle the Lord prompted us to start a fellowship group for the Indian community in the area and which continues to this day.

"I am the Lord, the God of all mankind. Is anything too hard for me?" Jeremiah 32:27. My response and experience to this is, 'No Lord, there is nothing too hard for Thee'. The amazing grace of God was always upon me, for example: 1) To preserve me when a violent storm and whirlwind came during my voyage by ship to the UK in 1959. 2) To help overcome my language difficulty, and reach a level to teach in English and to write books. 3) To raise me from sick bed to minister to many – through prayer, counselling, healing, teaching and preaching the Word of God for the past 21 years, among other things. 4) Despite my early retirement on medical grounds, we as a family lacked nothing. 5) When I was confined to my sick bed, incapacitated, a voice came in a dazzling light into my room saying, 'By My grace you are blessed.' God has always kept His Word. Indeed, God has also blessed me with such a caring and God-fearing family.

There is still plenty to do as there is no retirement in the kingdom of God. I pray that this testimony will encourage you and bring honour and glory to God.

K. T. Koshy
2013

REFERENCES

Chapter 1: God's Invitation – the New Birth
1. Mears, Henrietta C. *What the Bible Is All About.* Regal Books, A Division of G. L. Publications, California (1953), Cited in p 388.

Chapter 2: A New Start – Baptism
1. Koshy, PJT. *Baptism.* International Harvest Church, Newcastle, Church Bulletin, June 2010.

Chapter 3: God's Power for Living – the Holy Spirit
1. Wiersbe, Warren W. *Bible Commentary New Testament.* Thomas Nelson, Inc. Nashville (1991), cited in p 122.

Chapter 9: Jesus Christ Is Lord
1. Bob Gass. *Who Is Jesus?* UCB Word for Today, Stock-on-Trent, December 2010.

2. Mears, Henrietta C. *What the Bible Is All About.* Regal Books, A Division of G. L. Publications, California (1953), p 521.

Chapter 10: The Trinity.

1. Grudem, W. *Systematic Theology: An Introduction to Biblical Doctrine.* Inter-Varsity Press, Leicester, p 251.

2. Hocking, C. E. et al (Editors). *Day by Day through the Old Testament.* Precious Seed Publications, Trowbridge (1982), p 252.

Chapter 11: The Love of God

1. Campolo, Tony. *It's Friday But Sunday's Coming.* WORD (UK) Ltd, Herts (1985), p 68.

2. Matthew Henry. *Matthew Henry's Concise Commentary on the Whole Bible.* Thomas Nelson, Inc., Nashville (1997), p 984.

3. Lehman, Frederick M. *History of Song, the Love of God* (1948). Pink, A. W. The Attributes of God – The Love of God. Providence Baptist Ministries (2004), pp 1-5 (General reference).

Chapter 13: The Word of God – the Bible

1. Bob Gass. *The Word of God.* UCB Word for Today, Stoke-on-Trent.

2. Hayford, Jack W. (General Editor). *Kingdom Dynamic: Jesus and the Holy Scriptures, the Word of God.* Spirit Filled Life Bible, New King James Version. Thomas Nelson, Inc., Nashville 1991), pp 1547-48.

Chapter 14: Power of Prayer

1. Marsh, F. E. *1000 Bible Study Outlines.* Authentic Books, Andhra Pradesh (2000), p 310.

Chapter 15: Thanksgiving, Praise and Worship

1. Derek Prince. *Thanksgiving, Praise and Worship.* Nelson Word Ltd, Milton Keynes (1991), p 31.

Chapter 16: Who Am I in Christ
1. Kaseman, Jim. *Making Our Redemption a Reality* Article, Jim Kaseman Ministries, Oklahoma.

Chapter 17: The Lord's Supper
1. Hayford, Jack W. (General Editor). *Kingdom Dynamic: Faith at the Lord's Table*, Faith's Confession. Spirit Filled Life Bible, New King James Version. Thomas Nelson, Inc., Nashville (1991), p 1735.
2. Lunt, J. Mustard Seed Music (1978).

Chapter 18: The Ministry of the Church
1. The Holy Bible, New International Version, 1984 – We are not alone (no page number given), International Bible Society, United Kingdom.

Chapter 19: Marriage and Family Life
1. Norridge, G & M. *Marriage Matters*. Salt and Light Ministries, Oxford (2007), p 17.

Chapter 20: The Gifts and the Fruit of the Holy Spirit
1. Derek Prince. *Rules of Engagement*. Derek Prince Ministries – UK (2006), p 120.

Chapter 21: Divine Healing
1. Jones, Beth A. *Getting a Grip on the Basics of Health and Healing*. Valley Press Publications, Portage, MI (1995), p 84.

Chapter 23: The Second Coming of Jesus
1. Wiersbe, Warren W. *New Testament Bible Commentary*, Thomas Nelson Publishers, Nashville (1991), p 37.
2. Brown, R. Collins. *Gem Bible Guide*, Harper Collins Publishers, Glasgow (1993), p 290.

BIBLIOGRAPHY
(SELECTED)

Barclay, William. *Crucified and Crowned*. Arthur James Ltd, London (1988).

Barclay, William. *The Mind of Jesus*. Arthur James Ltd, London (1989).

Bosworth, F. F. *Christ The Healer*. Fleming H. Revell, A Division of Baker Book Rapids, Michigan (1924).

Clapham, D. et al (editors). *Day by Day through the New Testament*. Precious Seed Publications, W. Glam (1979).

Derek Prince. *Foundations for Righteous Living*. Derek Prince Ministries, UK (1998).

Duininck, G. *Grace for Effectual Ministry*. Master's Touch Ministries, Tulsa, Oklahoma (2011).

Hayford, Jack W. (General Editor). *Spirit-Filled Life Bible*, New King James Version. Thomas Nelson Publishers, Nashville (1991).

Hocking, C. *Day by Day Moments with the Master.* Precious Seed Publications, W. Glam (1994).

Holy Bible: The Open Bible, Expanded Edition, New American Standard Bible. World Publishing, a division of Thomas Nelson, Inc. Nashville (1985).

Holy Bible, New International Version, Thompson Chain Reference Edition. Hodder & Stoughton, London (1984).

Jones, Beth A. *Getting a Grip on the Basics of Health and Healing.* Valley Press Publications, Portage, MI (1995).

Jones, Beth A. *Getting a Grip on the Basics: Building a Firm Foundation for the Victorious Christian Life.* Harrison House, Oklahoma (1994).

Life Application Study Bible, New International Version. Tyndale House Publishers, Inc., Illinois and Zondervan Publishing House, Michigan (1991).

Mears, Henrietta C. *What the Bible Is All About.* Regal Books, A Division of GL Publications, California (1953).

Warren, Rick. *The Purpose-Driven Church.* Zondervan, Michigan (1995).

Wiersbe, Warren W. *Bible Commentary Old Testament.* Thomas Nelson, Inc. Nashville (1991).

Wommack, Andrew. *You've Already Got It!* Andrew Wommack Ministries (Europe), Walsall (2007).

About the author. . .

K. T. Koshy and his wife, Mary, have been actively serving the Lord for over 25 years, both in the UK and abroad. They currently live in Newcastle upon Tyne, where they are part of International Harvest Church Newcastle and founders of Newcastle Christian Fellowship, which works amongst the Indian community in the area. Previously they were co-leaders of a church plant in the south of England and have been engaged in various church building projects in India. They are marked by genuine love for both the Lord and people, and are recognised by many, including pastors and leaders, as parental figures in their lives. Koshy has been used extensively by the Lord in teaching God's Word, and both of them have ministered to numerous people, both practically and spiritually, with a concern to see people enjoy the love, freedom and life that Jesus has purchased for them. Koshy previously worked as Senior Lecturer at the London University of Greenwich, taught numerous NHS nursing students over a period of 25 years and has authored books and articles in his professional capacity.

NOTES

NOTES

NOTES